ANGER UNMASKED FOR PARENTS

ANGER UNMASKED FOR PARENTS

DISCOVERING THE HIDDEN PATH TO ANGER MANAGEMENT FOR HAPPY PARENTING AND RAISING PEACEFUL KIDS

SARAH THOMPSON

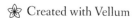

CONTENTS

FREE GIFT

To help you along your parenting journey, I've created this FREE companion resource to the book.

You can get instant access to the Anger Unmasked for Parents **Personal Workbook** by either clicking the link or scanning the QR code below.

This bonus is 100% free with no strings attached. You don't need to provide any personal information except your email address (so that I can send it to you).

This interactive workbook allows you to put the theory into practice and tailor your anger management strategies to your specific needs and circumstances.

To get your bonus, go to:

subscribe.reprynted.com/anger-unmasked-bonus

Or scan the QR code below

1. Anger Trigger Logs: Will help you identify your personal anger triggers and understand how they affect your emotional and physical responses.

2. Emotional Regulation Techniques: Provides detailed step-by-step instructions to techniques like deep breathing, progressive muscle relaxation.

3. Communication Exercises: Practice your effective communication, active listening, and conflict resolution skills with role-play scenarios and script-writing exercises.

4. Self-Care Planner: Templates for scheduling self-care activities and tracking habits, promoting a balanced emotional well-being.

5. Reflection and Journaling Prompts: Questions and prompts to encourage introspection about your experiences with anger, progress made, and areas for further improvement.

INTRODUCTION

I remember it like it was yesterday. I was standing in my kitchen, a sea of unsorted laundry on one side, an overflowing sink of dirty dishes on the other. My youngest, Ben, was tugging at my leg, his face stained with the remnants of lunch and tears. His continuous wailing was the soundtrack to my mounting frustration.

My two older kids, Lily and Max, were in the living room, a heated argument about a misplaced toy escalating to World War III levels. Their raised voices echoed through the house, adding to the cacophony of noise that was our typical afternoon.

I could feel it—the burning frustration, the overwhelming sense of being pulled in a million directions, the bubbling anger just beneath the surface. I took a deep breath, trying to steady the chaos within me. It was like trying to stop a tidal wave with paper.

I snapped.

"Enough!"

I shouted, my voice louder and harsher than I'd intended. The room fell into an unnerving silence. Ben's crying ceased abruptly, his wide, shocked eyes looking up at me. Lily and Max peeked around the corner, their faces reflecting a similar mix of surprise and fear.

I stood there, heart pounding, my own words echoing in my ears. I looked at their frightened faces, and it was like looking into a mirror reflecting the truth I'd been avoiding—I had let my anger control me, and it was affecting the people I loved most.

That moment was my wake-up call. It was the moment I realized that my anger, this uninvited guest, was no longer just an occasional visitor. It had moved in, set up shop, and was influencing my interactions with my children.

But along with the shock and guilt, there was something else—a glimmer of understanding. I realized that this anger wasn't born from the chaos of that particular moment or from my children's behavior. It was coming from a deeper place within me—a place of exhaustion, of feeling overwhelmed and unsupported, of unresolved issues and unaddressed emotions.

That's when I knew I had to make a change. I didn't want to be the parent who reacted out of anger. I didn't want to teach my children that love and anger were two sides of the same coin. I wanted to understand my anger, to learn how to manage it, to transform it from a destructive force into a catalyst for personal growth.

I have three incredible kids, each with their own vibrant personalities and unique ways of testing my patience. Just like you, I've been through the wringer of parenthood. I've cheered for my kids' victories, soothed their sorrows, and yes, lost my temper more times than I'd like to admit. This book is born out of my personal experience—my trek through the tricky terrain of parental anger, and the path I discovered towards understanding and emotional freedom.

Parenthood, as you well know, is a wild ride. It's a whirlwind of laughter, tears, joy, worry, pride, and frustration. One moment, you're on cloud nine as your child wraps their little arms around your neck, and the next, you're biting back words of anger as they test your boundaries yet again. If you've ever felt that anger bubbling up and wondered, "Is it just me?" I want you to know—you're not alone. We've all been there, and it's okay. This book is here to help.

This book is much more than words on paper—it's a roadmap born from my personal experiences, years of research, and a lot of introspection. The goal? To guide you as you navigate your own anger, understand its roots, and discover a sense of emotional freedom for both you and your family. Think of this book as a friendly companion, someone who's been down this road before and is ready to share everything they've learned.

May this book serves as your compass in the often-turbulent sea of parental emotions. From my own experience, I've learned that understanding anger isn't a quick fix—it's a transformative process that changes how we perceive our feelings, how we react to challenging situations, and ultimately, how we interact with our loved ones.

By engaging with this book, you will:

Gain a Deeper Understanding of Your Anger: Through personal anecdotes, research insights, and introspective exercises, you'll learn to identify the root causes of your anger, discerning the difference between surface triggers and deeper, underlying issues. This understanding is the first step toward emotional freedom.

Develop Effective Anger Management Techniques: You'll learn practical, actionable strategies to manage your anger in the moment. From breathing techniques and mindfulness practices to cognitive behavioral strategies, you'll equip yourself with a toolkit to navigate angry feelings and reactions.

Transform Your Relationship with Anger: This book will help you reframe your perspective on anger. Instead of seeing it as a destructive force, you'll learn to view it as a signal—a guide that can help you identify your unmet needs and advocate for yourself and your children in healthier ways.

Cultivate Stronger Relationships: By understanding and managing your anger, you'll foster more open, honest, and empathetic communication with your children. You'll become a model of emotional intelligence for your family, leading to stronger, more trusting relationships.

Empower Yourself: This is as much about personal growth as it is about parenting. By uncovering and addressing your anger, you'll foster self-awareness, compassion, and resilience. You'll empower yourself to face not only parental challenges, but any life situation with grace and understanding.

Achieve Emotional Freedom: Ultimately, the goal of this book is to guide you towards emotional freedom. This freedom comes from understanding your emotions, not fearing them. It comes from the ability to navigate life's ups and downs without being overwhelmed by anger. It's the freedom to fully enjoy the precious moments of parenthood, and the peace of mind that comes from knowing you're doing your best for your children and for yourself.

This is more than just a guide—it's an invitation to transform your life as a parent. It's a promise that while the journey may be challenging, the rewards of emotional freedom, self-understanding, and stronger family bonds are worth the effort. And remember, you're not alone. I'm here with you, sharing my experiences, insights, and support as you navigate your path to understanding and managing your anger.

The Elephant in the Room: Why Anger Management Matters

Sometimes, anger feels like the uninvited guest at the parenting party. It's that emotion we'd rather not admit to, especially when it's directed at the little people we love more than anything. But here's the truth—recognizing and managing our anger is vital. It's not just about avoiding the guilt that comes after a heated moment; it's about ensuring the emotional health of our families. When we can understand and navigate our anger, we can use it as a compass, guiding us towards better communication, stronger relationships, and a healthier family dynamic.

How we handle our anger as parents can leave a lasting imprint on our kids. In my course to understand anger, I came across some research that really made me pause. Studies from institutions like the American Psychological Association and Harvard Medical School suggest that children exposed to frequent, intense expressions of parental anger can potentially develop emotional challenges such as anxiety disorders, depression, and struggles with self-esteem and social relationships. It was a sobering moment for me, realizing the deep influence our emotional state can have on our little ones.

As a parent, we often see anger as a negative force, something to be suppressed or avoided. But here's an uncommon belief that I've come to embrace: our anger, when understood and managed effectively, can serve as a powerful catalyst for personal growth and positive change.

In our society, anger is often regarded as a destructive force. But what if we could flip the script? What if we could see our anger not as a villain, but as a guide, pointing us towards areas in our lives that need attention or change?

We'll be doing just that. We'll look at anger not as the enemy, but as a messenger, carrying valuable information about our unmet needs, unresolved issues, and personal boundaries.

Before we dive in, let's talk about how we'll approach this adventure. As you flip through these pages, I want you to remember one thing: this isn't about striving for perfection. There's no such thing as a perfect parent— we're all wonderfully human, after all. This is about growth and understanding. It's about having the courage to look inward, even when it's uncomfortable, and having the grace to forgive ourselves when we stumble.

In the coming chapters, we'll walk through the various stages of understanding and managing anger. We'll delve into its roots, explore strategies for calming the storm when it hits, discuss the power of forgiveness, and much more. We'll share stories, explore insights, and learn practical tools that have helped me and countless others. Each chapter is a stepping stone towards a deeper understanding of your anger and how to manage it effectively.

So, my friend, are you ready to embark on this quest with me? To peel back the layers, face the discomfort, and uncover the emotional freedom that lies beneath? Change isn't easy, but it's worth it. And I'll be with you every step of the way, sharing my experiences, my triumphs, and yes, my failures too. Because that's what this is all about — not just learning from textbooks and studies, but learning from each other.

The Nitty-Gritty of Emotions: Why Understanding Anger is Crucial

I believe it's important we take a moment to talk about why understanding anger is so vital. Anger is often stigmatized and avoided, seen as a destructive force we'd rather not confront. But the truth is, anger is not the enemy. It's a normal, natural emotion that carries valuable information about our needs and boundaries. The problem arises when we let anger control us, instead of us controlling it. It's like a fire—useful when controlled, but destructive when it runs wild. By understanding our anger, we can learn to use its energy constructively and avoid the potential harm it can cause if left unchecked.

Skeptics might say that anger is a natural and unavoidable emotion, that it is part of our human nature, and managing it might seem like suppressing one's true feelings. They might argue that it's not the anger that's the problem, but rather how we react to it. They may view the process of digging into past traumas, unresolved issues, and unmet needs as unnecessary, believing instead that people should focus on the present and future rather than dwelling on the past. They may also question the effectiveness of anger management techniques, suggesting that they are merely temporary solutions that don't address the root causes of anger. They may even believe that expressing anger openly and without restraint is healthier and more authentic than attempting to manage or control it.

Throughout your reading, you'll be doing a lot of digging. Like archaeologists, you'll explore the layers of your emotions, going beyond the surface anger to the feelings and experiences that lie beneath. You'll look at past traumas, unresolved issues, and unmet needs. It might be uncomfortable at times, but it's through this exploration that you can truly understand your anger and how to manage it effectively.

If you're concerned that anger is a natural and unavoidable emotion, you're absolutely right. I completely agree with you. Anger is indeed a natural emotion and we all experience it. But the issue isn't about avoiding anger; it's about managing it. This book helps you learn to express your anger healthily, without causing harm to yourself or others. It's not about suppressing your anger, but navigating it in a way that leads to personal growth and better relationships.

For those of you who feel it's not the anger that's the problem, but our reaction to it, I'd say you're halfway there! That's exactly what we're going to explore in this book. We're diving deep into understanding our reactions, and more importantly, learning how to respond to anger in a constructive way rather than reacting impulsively.

And to those who find the idea of revisiting past traumas and unmet needs uncomfortable, I hear you. It's not an easy process, and I acknowledge your apprehensions. However, it's through understanding these underlying factors that we gain the power to break free from destructive patterns. Remember, this book is your safe space, guiding you to face those emotions at your own pace. It's not about forcing you into discomfort, but gently helping you to understand your anger's roots and how to heal.

Lastly, to those who think this all sounds like a lot of work, I won't sugarcoat it—it is. But believe me when I say, the payoff is enormous. Effective anger management isn't a quick fix; it's a continuous process of learning and growing. But with this book, you're not alone. I'm with you every step of the way, providing the tools and strategies you need to manage your anger effectively. The investment is worth the reward: a life free from the chains of uncontrolled anger.

As you delve deeper, it's crucial to remember that this is all about progress. There's no quick fix or magic solution. Managing anger is a process, and it takes time. But with patience, self-compassion, and a willingness to learn, we can make significant strides. And remember, it's okay to stumble. It's okay to have moments of frustration or confusion. That's all part of change and achieving success. What's important is that we keep going, keep learning, and keep growing.

An Open Heart: The Power of Forgiveness and Letting Go

One of the most transformative steps you will be learning is to forgive. Forgiveness, both towards others and towards ourselves, is a powerful tool in managing anger. It doesn't mean forgetting or excusing hurtful behavior, but rather releasing the anger and resentment that keeps us stuck. It's about letting go of the past so we can move forward with peace and emotional freedom.

Another key aspect we'll explore is communication. How we express our anger can significantly impact our relationships, especially with our children. We'll delve into strategies for assertive communication, active listening, and conflict resolution, all aimed at fostering a stronger connection with our children and teaching them how to express their own feelings in a healthy, constructive way.

As you come to understand your anger better, you can begin to see it in a new light. Rather than a destructive force, it can become a catalyst for positive change. You can learn to channel your anger towards advocating for your needs, setting healthy boundaries, and fostering personal growth. We'll explore this concept further, transforming how we perceive and handle our anger.

Self-Care Isn't Selfish: Prioritizing Your Well-being

Last but not least, you'll delve into the importance of self-care. As parents, we often put ourselves last, but to manage our anger effectively, we need to prioritize our well-being. This doesn't mean lavish spa days or expensive retreats (although those are nice!). It's about carving out time for rest, for activities that rejuvenate us, and for practices that help us maintain a balanced emotional state. We'll delve into various self-care strategies, from mindfulness and meditation to physical exercise and maintaining social connections. You'll learn that taking care of ourselves is not a luxury—it's a necessity.

This book is for every parent who has ever felt the surge of anger and wondered, "Is there a better way?" It's for those who have lost their temper and then been consumed by guilt. It's for the moms and dads who are desperate for a moment of peace amid the chaos of parenthood, yet find themselves reacting in ways they regret. This book is for the parents who love their children deeply but are overwhelmed by the intensity of their emotions. It's for those who are ready to break the cycle of anger and step into a new way of relating with their children. No matter where you are in your parenting life—whether you're a new parent just starting out, or a seasoned veteran navigating the teen years—this book is for you. It's a tool, a guide, and a companion for anyone ready to understand their anger, transform their reactions, and foster healthier, stronger relationships with their children.

Remember that it's not about achieving perfection, but progress. We're all beautifully imperfect beings, and our mistakes and missteps are opportunities for growth. Embrace the imperfections, and celebrate the small victories along the way. Every step you take, no matter how small, is a testament to your courage and commitment.

Are you tired of feeling guilty after losing your cool? Do you find yourself lying in bed at night, replaying the day's heated moments and wishing for a do-over? Are you ready for a change, ready to replace the cycle of anger and guilt with understanding and compassion? Do you yearn for more peaceful interactions with your children, for a home environment that is a sanctuary of calm instead of a battleground of emotions? Perhaps you've tried other methods, read other books, attended workshops, but you're still struggling with the same issues. If you're seeking a deeper understanding of your anger, a way to address not just the symptoms but the root causes, this book is for you. It's a guide for parents who are ready to embark on a transformative odyssey, to uncover the hidden triggers of their anger, and discover healthier, more effective ways to express their emotions and engage with their children. If you're eager to move from the realm of reactions to the realm of understanding, from guilt to forgiveness, from turmoil to tranquility, this book is your next step.

But it doesn't end when you turn the last page of this book—it continues every day of your lives. The tools and strategies you'll learn are not just for now, but for your lifelong progress of personal growth and emotional health.

It's not an easy path, but it's a worthwhile one. And remember, you're not alone—I'm here with you, and so are countless other parents who are walking this path. So, are you ready? Ready to unmask your anger, understand its roots, and discover the path to emotional freedom? If so, let's begin. The quest is yours, and it starts now.

1

EMBRACING THE FIRE

MY JOURNEY INTO THE REALM OF PARENTAL ANGER

As an author and a mother of three, I've worn the same shoes you're wearing now. Parenting is often navigating the tumultuous waters of anger. The frustration, the guilt, the sheer exhaustion—it's an experience I'm intimately familiar with. I've spent countless nights questioning my actions, wondering if there was a better way I could have responded, a more patient tone I could have adopted, a kinder word I could have spoken.

If you've picked up this book, chances are, you've known what it's like to feel the hot rush of anger while dealing with your child. Perhaps you've experienced that sinking feeling of regret that sets in afterward. Maybe you've even felt a sense of isolation, thinking that you're the only parent struggling with such intensity of anger. I want to extend my hand to you across these pages and assure you—you're not alone.

Every parent has been there, feeling the sting of anger, the weight of guilt, and the tug of exhaustion. There are days when the challenges seem endless, when the pressures of parenting press down upon us relentlessly. Maybe you've felt the silent judgement of society, the expectation to always be patient, always be nurturing, always be in control of your emotions. It can be overwhelming, and I want you to know that it's okay to feel this way.

Through this book, I want to acknowledge the raw, real emotions that come with parenting, including the anger. More importantly, I want to offer you strategies, insight, and compassion. I want to offer you a space where your feelings are acknowledged and understood, where your struggles are seen, and where you can find the tools to navigate them. You have support. I'm right here with you, and together, we'll learn how to better understand and manage our parental anger.

A Glimpse into My World

In our home, the day often reaches a crescendo around 5 pm, what I've come to refer to as the *witching hour*. It's the point when my kids, weary from a day of schoolwork and cooped up energy, burst into a frenzy just as I'm attempting to prepare dinner. I remember one evening in particular that stands out in my memory. My middle child, in a whirl of laughter and giddy chaos, accidentally knocked over a glass of milk.

It cascaded across the counter in slow motion, splattering the freshly folded laundry I had optimistically placed there. In that moment, the dam of my patience burst. I yelled, my face hot, my heart pounding, my voice echoing around the suddenly silent kitchen. I was more like a raging volcano than the calm, composed parent I aspired to be. In the wake of my eruption, the room fell silent, and I was left standing amidst the stillness with a churning stomach and a heavy heart.

These moments of anger weren't isolated incidents. They were sporadic yet recurring reminders of the battle I was fighting with myself—my desire to be a patient, understanding parent eclipsed by my own anger. It was a cycle of remorse and frustration. I'd lose my temper, then find myself awash with guilt, wondering why I had let myself react so vehemently. The emotional toll was not just on me but also on my children. I could see the confusion in their eyes, their smiles fading, replaced by a hesitant wariness.

There's another particular incident that has ingrained itself deep within my memory. It was an ordinary Saturday morning. The sun was barely up, and the aroma of brewing coffee wafted through the house, a promise of the peaceful weekend morning that I was anticipating. My youngest, a spirited toddler at the time, was engaged in a relentless pursuit of the family cat. The laughter-filled chase was abruptly halted when the cat, in its bid for freedom, leaped onto the kitchen table, knocking over my just-poured, steaming cup of coffee onto a pile of school projects that my eldest had painstakingly completed the night before.

The trigger was pulled again, and I felt the familiar rush of heat, the volcanic rumble of anger welling up inside me. I tried not to yell, but I couldn't help it, my voice harsh and jarring against the hush of the early morning. My toddler, startled, began to cry. My eldest, wide-eyed and upset, stared at the ruined projects on the table. And there I stood, the epicenter of the storm, my heart pounding and my guilt surging as I looked at the fallout of my outburst.

Instances like these were not rare. There were many days when I felt like I was walking a tightrope, teetering between the pressure of being a *good* parent and the reality of my anger. The guilt I felt after each outburst was overwhelming. It was a painful reminder of the gap between the parent I wanted to be and the parent I was in those moments.

I share these personal stories not to wallow in past guilt, but to extend a hand of camaraderie to you. I want to tell you that I understand the frustration, the guilt, the sheer exhaustion that can come from dealing with parental anger. I've spent countless nights questioning my actions, replaying situations, and wondering if I could have done things differently.

But here's the thing: you're not alone in these feelings. And these experiences, as challenging as they are, can be powerful catalysts for change. They were for me. Each instance of anger became a stepping stone, a lesson that nudged me towards seeking a better understanding of my emotions, and ultimately, finding ways to manage them. If you're reading this, I want to reassure you that it's okay to struggle. It's okay to have these moments. What matters is that we acknowledge them, learn from them, and take steps towards positive change.

I share these stories not to burden you with my guilt but to connect with your experiences. I want to create a bridge of understanding, a common ground where you can see your struggles mirrored in mine. I've been there too. I've felt the searing rush of anger, the heavy cloak of guilt, and the longing for change. But more importantly, I want to assure you that you're not alone, and there is a way forward. These instances, as hard as they were, served as my motivation to understand and manage my anger better, and I hope they serve as a beacon of shared experience for you, too.

Parenting Anger is Universal

Parenting is like walking a high wire; it's an intense, high-stakes endeavor where the pressures and challenges can often lead to frustration and anger. This is a universal truth, a shared flame that burns within all of us as we navigate the uncharted waters of raising our children. It's a rarely discussed part of parenting, hidden under layers of societal expectations and norms. As parents, we are often expected to be endlessly patient, selfless, and composed. The relentless demands of our role—the sleepless nights, the endless chores, the constant mental juggling of schedules and needs—can ignite feelings of anger. It's natural. It's human. And it's okay.

The world we live in often paints an unrealistic picture of parenthood. It pressures us to maintain a calm facade, to suppress our frustrations, and meet the unending demands of parenting with a constant smile. This can lead to feelings of isolation and shame when we inevitably experience anger. It's as if we are failing in our roles because we can't uphold this impossible standard of perpetual serenity. But I want you to know that it's okay to feel overwhelmed, it's okay to feel angry, and it's okay to feel exhausted.

These feelings don't make you a bad parent; they make you a human one. Your feelings are valid. They are a testament to the love and effort you pour into your role every single day. What matters is not that we experience anger, but how we understand it, how we handle it, and how we learn from it.

I want you to remember, as you turn each page of this book, that you are not alone. There are millions of parents out there grappling with the same emotions, experiencing the same struggles. We are all in this together, each of us trying to do the best we can for our children, and each of us learning as we go. There is a shared strength in this universality, a shared understanding that we are all doing our best in a complex and demanding role. So, let's explore together, unearthing the roots of our anger, and finding healthier, more productive ways to manage it.

Anger Unveiled: An Insight into Its Nature

To truly manage our anger, we must first seek to understand it. Anger is like a fire. If we understand its nature, how it starts, what fuels it, and how it spreads, we can better control it, prevent it from causing harm, and even use it to our advantage. This understanding is the cornerstone of our trip towards managing parental anger.

At its core, anger is a physiological response—a survival mechanism that primes our bodies for action in the face of a perceived threat. It triggers a surge of adrenaline, quickening our heartbeat and sharpening our senses, preparing us for the primal "fight or flight" response. While this response served our ancestors well, allowing them to react swiftly to physical threats, it can lead to destructive behaviors in the modern, relational context of parenting. The perceived threats we now face are often emotional or psychological, and the *fight or flight* response is often inappropriate and counterproductive.

But anger is more than just a physiological response; it's also a psychological signal. It's often the tip of an emotional iceberg, a visible manifestation of deeper, hidden feelings—fear, frustration, or hurt. Just as an iceberg's true size and shape are hidden beneath the surface, the true nature and cause of our anger are often concealed, buried under layers of unaddressed emotions and unresolved issues. When we start to see our anger not as an enemy to be feared or suppressed, but as a messenger alerting us to these deeper emotions, we begin to reclaim control. We can start to address the root causes of our anger, rather than just battling its symptoms.

One of the most critical insights I've had in my parenting life so far was realizing the crucial distinction between feeling angry and acting destructively because of anger. The former is a natural emotion, a universal human experience. The latter is a behavior, a response to that emotion. And while we can't always control our feelings (nor should we try to), we can control our behaviors. We can choose how we respond to our anger. This realization was a turning point for me. It empowered me to take ownership of my responses, to channel my anger in healthier, more constructive ways.

This is key: not to eliminate anger—that's neither possible nor desirable—but to understand it, to listen to what it's telling us, and to learn to express it in ways that do not harm ourselves or the ones we love. By understanding the nature of anger, we take the first crucial step towards changing how we interact with this powerful emotion.

Harnessing Anger for Growth

As I went deeper into the heart of my anger, I began to understand its transformative potential. This wasn't a path I embarked on willingly—at least, not at first. It felt more like a forced march, driven by necessity rather than choice. But as I ventured further, I started to see the landscape of my emotions with new clarity.

In examining my triggers—the specific situations or behaviors that sparked my anger—I found that they were like signposts, pointing me towards hidden aspects of myself that needed attention. Each flare-up of anger was a beacon illuminating insecurities and fears I didn't know I harbored. It was as if my anger was a lantern, casting light into the dark corners of my emotional world, revealing parts of myself that I had overlooked or neglected.

As I began working through these newly uncovered emotions, I felt a profound sense of liberation. It was as if I'd been carrying a heavy backpack, its weight steadily growing over the years, and I was finally allowed to set it down. This didn't make it easier—quite the opposite. It made me realize just how hard I had been working to carry that burden and how much energy I had been wasting. But this realization was liberating. It gave me hope. It made me believe that change was possible.

The road to managing parental anger is not an easy one. It's a path that winds through challenging terrain, across the landscapes of our past experiences, our deeply held beliefs, and our most vulnerable emotions. But I assure you, it's a journey worth taking.

That transformed not just my relationship with my children, but also my relationship with myself. It's given me greater self-awareness, enabling me to recognize and respond to my emotions in healthier ways. It's taught me patience, allowing me to navigate stressful situations with more grace. And perhaps most importantly, it's deepened my sense of compassion—for my children, for other parents going through similar struggles, and for myself.

My hope is that, through this book, you'll be inspired to begin your own transformation. I hope that you'll find the courage to explore your anger, to understand it, and to harness its energy for growth. Because while anger can be destructive, it can also be a powerful catalyst for change. It can be a tool for self-discovery, a compass guiding you towards a healthier, happier version of yourself. And that's well worth the effort.

Igniting the Path Forward

And so, I extend an invitation to you: embark on this journey with me. Commit to unpacking the suitcase of your anger, to thawing the frozen layers of your emotional iceberg. It's not an easy task—I won't sugarcoat that reality—but it's an undeniably valuable one. The transformation that results from understanding and addressing anger is profound, leading to a more peaceful and harmonious family dynamic.

In the chapters that follow, we'll provide you with a toolbox filled with practical strategies to manage your anger. We'll venture into the dark forest of emotional triggers, unmask hidden emotions that lurk behind your anger, and equip you with the means to express your anger in a healthy, constructive way.

We'll uncover the power of forgiveness, not just towards others, but towards ourselves. We'll underscore the importance of effective communication in managing anger and its role in fostering a healthier, more understanding relationship with your children. And ultimately, we'll explore how to channel anger as a force for personal growth, enabling you to transform your relationship with this powerful emotion.

Please, remember: this process is a marathon, not a sprint. It takes time. There will be days when you stumble, moments when you question your progress, or even your ability to change. On those days, be gentle with yourself. Every step you take, no matter how small it seems, is progress. It's a step towards becoming a more understanding, patient, and emotionally aware parent. And that's something to be proud of.

And so, here we stand, on the precipice of this trip. Take my hand. Let's step forward into this brave new world of understanding and managing parental anger together. Let's venture onto this path of emotional freedom and harmonious family life. Because if there's one thing I've learned throughout my own parenting life, it's that change is possible. And it starts with a single step.

Remember, you are not by yourself. I'm here with you, every step of the way. Together, we can navigate the challenges, celebrate the victories, and support each other when it gets tough. We can take this step together —for ourselves, for our families, for the peaceful homes we yearn to create.

This is more than just a path to managing anger—it's a way towards a happier, healthier, more fulfilling life as a parent. So let's take that first step together. Let's ignite the path forward.

2

PEELING BACK THE LAYERS
UNMASKING THE ROOTS OF YOUR ANGER

That time in the kitchen still sticks in my memory like a stubborn piece of gum on a shoe. There I was, standing amidst the usual kitchen mess, feeling my blood boil and my cheeks flush. Despite my best "keep calm" mantra playing on repeat in my head, my voice was on a roller coaster ride, going up and up. It was like a broken record, this scene, one that had played out way too many times. And I couldn't help but wonder, "Why the heck does this keep happening?"

So, that's what this chapter is all about. We're here to crack the code, to get to the bottom of this anger mystery, for both you and me. It's like we're detectives, trying to uncover the clues about our anger, figure out where it comes from, and how we can get a handle on it.

Think about it like we're gardening. A gardener doesn't just chuck some seeds in the dirt and hope for the best, right? They need to know the nitty-gritty about the soil, the weather, and what each plant needs to bloom. That's how we need to approach this whole anger business. We need to dig deep and understand our emotions to create a happier, more chilled out family life.

So, let's get our hands dirty and dive right in. We'll peel back the layers of our emotions, figure out our triggers, and make sense of our past experiences. Sure, it might feel a bit rough around the edges sometimes, but trust me, it'll be worth it. By understanding our anger, we'll be able to connect better with our kids, our partners, and heck, even with ourselves.

So, ready to roll up your sleeves and start this exploration? Let's do this together!

Unearthing the Past: How Our History Shapes Our Anger

Here's the thing: our past is like this huge, overstuffed suitcase that we lug around, whether we like it or not. It's filled to the brim with all our experiences, lessons we've learned, and beliefs we've picked up along the way. Sometimes, we don't even realize how heavy it's gotten until we start to unpack it.

As I started rummaging through my own past, I discovered that a lot of my anger bursts were linked to unresolved stuff and emotions from my kiddo days that I hadn't fully dealt with.

Let's spill some tea. You know that moment when your kid flat out refuses to eat their dinner? The frustration is real, right? I mean, how many different ways can you make a carrot interesting? But whenever this happened, I found myself blowing a fuse. I couldn't figure it out until I took a deep dive into my past.

Turns out, this dinner debacle was tied to my own experiences growing up. We didn't have a lot, and wasting food was a big no-no in our house. So, when my kids turned their noses up at their meals, it was like a punch to the gut. Once I made this connection, it was like someone turned on a light. I started handling these mealtime showdowns with a bit more understanding and patience.

But hey, don't get me wrong. I'm not saying all your past experiences are a bummer. Far from it. They're simply pieces of the puzzle that make you, well, you. They've shaped how you react to the world, including those moments when you might lose your cool as a parent.

So, my advice? Start unpacking that suitcase. Take a good look at your past, and you might just find the keys to understanding your present. And remember, we're in this together, friend. Unpacking isn't always easy, but it sure is worth it!

Buried Emotions: The Hidden Drivers of Anger

Think about emotions as this vast, intricate landscape within us. It's kind of like an archaeological dig site, filled with layers upon layers of buried artifacts - or in this case, feelings. As I traveled through my own emotional terrain, I stumbled upon a treasure trove of buried feelings that, surprise surprise, were the real culprits behind my bouts of anger.

These feelings - the fear, the guilt, the sadness, the frustration - they were all tucked away neatly, out of sight, like an underground reservoir. But, even buried, they had power. They were like a hidden wellspring, ready to surge up and spill over into anger at the slightest poke.

Here's a slice from my own life - I found that my anger-meter shot up when I felt overwhelmed or underappreciated. Connecting the dots, I realized that instead of dealing with these feelings straight up, I was letting them morph into anger. Spotting this pattern was like turning on a light in a dark room. It allowed me to face these emotions head-on, rather than getting lost in the heat of anger.

Now, how about you? What's buried in your emotional landscape? Are there feelings you've been brushing under the rug, feelings that are dressing up as anger? Remember, it's perfectly okay to feel these emotions.

They're not *evil twins* or unwanted guests. They're an integral part of our human experience.

So, why not take a moment to do some emotional archaeology? You might be surprised at what you discover about yourself. And remember, this isn't about judgment or blame. It's about understanding, about realizing that sometimes, anger is just a costume, a disguise worn by other emotions. And by recognizing this, we can begin to manage our reactions in a more conscious, compassionate way. So, are you ready to grab that metaphorical shovel and start digging?

Triggers and Patterns: Recognizing Your Anger Blueprint

Here's something I found out - we all have our unique anger blueprints. Think of it as a map that charts out our anger's triggers and patterns. If we can get a handle on this blueprint, it can become a seriously powerful tool in managing our reactions.

For me, it was like solving a mystery. I started paying attention to the moments when my anger was likely to flare up. What were the conditions that acted like sparks to my fuse? The answer was enlightening - lack of sleep, a chaotic home, and feeling unsupported were my prime suspects.

Let's take the cluttered home example. I noticed that when the house was a mess, my temper was on a hair-trigger. The kids' toys strewn around, dishes piling up in the sink, laundry mountain growing by the minute – it all added to a sense of chaos and loss of control, which, I realized, was a fast track to my anger station.

As I identified these triggers, it gave me a chance to prepare myself, to brace for the impact, so to speak. Instead of being caught off-guard, I could anticipate the wave of anger and manage my reactions better. I could consciously choose a calmer response, or better still, address the trigger before it had a chance to light my fuse.

What about you? What sets off your anger alarm? Are there specific situations, certain behaviors, or particular times of the day when your anger is more likely to show up? Could it be the morning rush of getting the kids ready for school? Or perhaps, it's the evening chaos when everyone's tired but there's still dinner to be made, homework to be done, and the kids to be settled into bed.

Recognizing these patterns, becoming aware of your anger's favorite hangouts, so to speak, can help you anticipate and navigate these challenging moments with more grace and effectiveness. It's like having a heads up on traffic jams and roadblocks, allowing you to navigate your emotional landscape more smoothly.

So, take some time to reflect, to uncover your own anger blueprint. Remember, this isn't about self-criticism but about self-awareness. The more we understand ourselves, the better we can navigate our emotional world, and the more effective we become in creating a harmonious family life.

The Reflective Mirror: Turning Inwards for Insight

I've got to tell you, one of the most game-changing tools I discovered in my quest to understand and manage my anger was self-reflection. It's like turning on a flashlight in a dark room. Suddenly, things that were hidden or overlooked become visible, and you gain a whole new perspective.

Self-reflection isn't about self-judgment or criticism. It's about observing our thoughts, emotions, and beliefs with kindness and curiosity. Imagine you're an explorer, setting off on an expedition into the uncharted territories of your inner world. You're not there to judge or change the landscape; you're there to understand it.

For me, this exploration took many forms - journaling, meditation, and quiet moments of introspection. Journaling became my personal think tank, a safe space to express, explore, and evaluate my feelings. It was like having a conversation with myself, but on paper. Meditating helped me quiet the noise and tune into my inner dialogue. It was like hitting the pause button on life's chaos and tapping into the calm beneath. And those quiet moments of introspection, often during a walk or a cup of tea, allowed me to reconnect with myself amidst the hustle and bustle of everyday life.

Now, I'd like to invite you to try this for yourself. Start with something simple. Maybe you could take a few minutes at the end of the day to jot down your thoughts and feelings. Or perhaps, you could try a short, guided meditation. There are plenty of free apps and online resources to get you started. And remember, there's no right or wrong way to do this. It's not about reaching a destination, but about the process of exploration and discovery.

As you embark on your self-reflection voyage, keep an open mind and a gentle heart. This isn't about fixing or changing anything; it's about understanding. It's about getting to know yourself better, about uncovering the layers of your emotions and beliefs, about recognizing the patterns that shape your reactions. The insights you'll gain can be transformative, helping you navigate your emotional world with greater awareness, understanding, and compassion.

Unraveling Personal Narratives: Challenging Your Beliefs About Anger

Have you ever noticed the stories we tell ourselves about our anger? We all have them. They're like well-worn paths in our minds that shape how we perceive and react to our emotions. For me, one of these stories was, "If I get angry, I'm a bad parent." It was as if I'd etched this belief into my psyche, and it was shaping my reactions, my guilt, and ultimately, my anger.

Let's hit the pause button here for a second. Why don't you think about the stories you're telling yourself about your anger? Are they helping you, or are they more like an anchor, weighing you down? Here's the thing: these stories, these beliefs - they're not set in stone. They're not unchangeable facts. They're narratives that we've created, and just like any story, they can be rewritten.

Unraveling these personal narratives requires a good dose of courage, a pinch of curiosity, and a healthy helping of self-compassion. It's not about judgment or self-criticism. It's about exploration and understanding. For me, this process started with a question: "Why do I believe that getting angry makes me a bad parent?" As I began to explore this, I realized that it was rooted in my own childhood experiences and societal expectations. It was a lightbulb moment that helped me see how this belief was fueling my guilt and amplifying my anger.

Now, I'd like to invite you to embark on a similar exploration. What beliefs are you holding onto about your anger? Where did they come from? How are they influencing your reactions? Remember, this isn't about finding fault or placing blame. It's about understanding and compassion. It's about rewriting those stories that no longer serve you and redefining your relationship with your anger.

The power to change these narratives lies within you. And the first step is recognizing them. So, grab a notebook, find a quiet space, and start exploring. You might be surprised by what you discover. Remember, this is a process, not a one-time event. Be patient with yourself. Keep an open mind and a gentle heart.

Embracing the Exploration: The Courage to Face Your Anger

Peeling back the layers of your anger isn't exactly a walk in the park. It's more like a hike through uncharted territory. It's challenging, it's messy, and sometimes, it's downright uncomfortable. I won't sugarcoat it - there were times in my own exploration when I wanted to pack it in. To put up a "closed for renovations" sign and call it a day. But every step I took towards understanding my anger, no matter how small, was a step towards emotional liberation.

So, here's my invitation to you: embrace this exploration. Yes, it can be tough. But it's also immensely empowering. By delving into the roots of your anger, you're not just unearthing your triggers and patterns. You're also discovering your strengths, your resilience, and your capacity for growth.

This isn't about reaching some magical destination where you'll never feel anger again. That's not realistic, and frankly, it's not the goal. Anger is a part of our human experience. The real goal here is understanding your anger, so you can navigate it with more awareness and kindness. It's about striving to be the kind of parent you aspire to be - not flawless, but present, genuine, and continually learning and growing.

When we start to unravel our anger, we can begin to loosen its hold on us. We can approach tricky situations with more empathy, respond to our triggers with a deeper understanding, and foster a more authentic connection with our kids. Every layer of anger we peel back is an opportunity for us to bloom into the parents we strive to be.

Self-discovery isn't for the faint of heart. It takes courage. It takes vulnerability. But believe me when I say that it's worth it. By understanding the roots of our anger, we can reclaim our power over it. We can become more present, more authentic, and more attuned to our children's needs. So, take a deep breath, muster up your courage, and dive in. You've got this.

Taking a Step Toward Self-Discovery

Remember, there's no rush in this process. It's okay to take your time. Uncovering the roots of your anger is not about quick fixes but about embarking on a transformative route of self-discovery. So, as you move forward, remember to be patient with yourself. Give yourself the space and time you need to reflect, process, and grow.

Understanding your anger is much like a hike through unknown territory. There will be challenging ascents, confusing crossroads, and perhaps even moments of wanting to turn back. But remember, every step you take is progress. You are moving forward. You are growing. And with each step, you are forging a path towards a more peaceful, harmonious family life.

At this point, you might be asking, "What's next?" Now that we've started to uncover the roots of our anger, how do we deal with it in the heat of the moment? How can we navigate the storm of our emotions when we're in the thick of it?

In the next chapter, we'll explore practical strategies for regulating our emotions when anger strikes. We'll talk about tools and techniques that can help us remain grounded in the midst of chaos, and ways to nurture a sense of calm within ourselves, even when our surroundings are anything but.

But for now, take a moment to appreciate yourself for learning about all this. By choosing to understand your anger, you're taking a powerful step towards emotional freedom. You're not just shaping your own life but also the lives of your children. And that, my friend, is something to be immensely proud of.

3

NAVIGATING THE STORM

PRACTICAL TOOLS FOR EMOTIONAL REGULATION

Let's face it. As parents, we've all had those moments when we feel like we're in the eye of a storm. The kids are squabbling, the house is a mess, and we're trying to juggle a million things at once. It's in these moments that our anger often catches us off-guard. This chapter is all about giving you practical, real-world tools to navigate these storms. Because, believe me, effective emotional regulation is your best ally in those challenging parenting moments.

Welcome to the exploration of managing anger in real-time as a parent. You've delved into the roots of your anger, but now we're shifting gears to look at how to handle it when it crops up in the heat of the moment. After all, understanding the why of your anger is only half the battle – dealing with it effectively when it happens is crucial. Imagine you're a sailor navigating stormy seas; understanding why the storm happens is useful, but what you really need is the skill to sail through it safely. And that's what we're focusing on in this chapter – your practical toolkit for emotional regulation.

As parents, we're bound to encounter challenging moments. The toddler throwing a tantrum in the grocery store, the teenager rolling their eyes at family dinner, or the sheer exhaustion of juggling work, family, and personal time. In these moments, the ability to maintain calm and composed can be a real game-changer. And this is where emotional regulation comes in. By cultivating these skills, you're preparing yourself to handle these parenting storms with grace, patience, and resilience.

My Go-To Strategies: Tips from the Trenches

As I navigated through the rocky terrain of parental anger, I stumbled upon a few strategies that turned out to be my life rafts in the tumultuous sea of emotions. They didn't come to me in a eureka moment; rather, they were the fruits of persistence, trial and error, and a whole lot of patience. So, let's dive into these tried-and-true strategies that have helped me keep my cool during those testing parenting moments.

The "pause and respond" method was one of my earliest discoveries and remains a staple in my toolbox. Picture this: Your child spills juice on your freshly cleaned carpet or refuses to do their homework despite repeated reminders. Feel that familiar heat of anger surging up? This is where you hit the pause button. Just a brief moment to take a deep breath, feeling the air fill your lungs and then slowly leave your body. This deliberate pause acts like a circuit breaker, disrupting the automatic surge of anger and giving you a chance to choose your response consciously.

But let me be clear, it's not about suppressing the anger. It's about giving yourself the space to experience the anger without letting it dictate your actions. So, instead of lashing out, you might choose to express your frustration calmly or decide to tackle the situation later when you're less heated. Remember, it's not about being a *perfect* parent who never gets angry; it's about being a *present* parent who can manage their emotions effectively.

Another strategy that has been a game-changer for me is what I call "shifting the lens." When I find myself stuck in a cycle of anger, I try to shift my perspective and see the situation through a different lens. For instance, instead of focusing on the mess my children have made while playing, I try to see the creativity and fun they had in the process. This shift doesn't dismiss my initial feelings of frustration, but it offers a broader perspective and helps me approach the situation with more understanding and less anger.

These strategies didn't come easily to me; they took time to develop and require ongoing practice. They may seem simple, but their power lies in their application. When used consistently, they can make a significant difference in the way you experience and express your anger.

However, it's crucial to remember that these strategies may not work for everyone in every situation. We all have our unique emotional makeup, and what works for me might not work for you. The key is to be open to experimenting, discovering what resonates with you, and crafting your own unique set of tools. Just remember, it's not about achieving perfection but progress, one mindful step at a time.

Inhale, Exhale: The Magic of Deep Breathing

Have you ever noticed how your breath becomes shallow and quick when you're angry? This is your body's automatic response to stress. But the good news is, you have the power to reverse this response through deep breathing. Deep breathing is like a secret magic trick that we all carry within us, a tool that can help us regain our balance during those emotionally intense moments.

Let's delve into one of my favourite breathing techniques, often referred to as *box breathing*. Picture a square box in your mind, with each side representing a step in the breathing process. Here's how you do it:

1. Close your eyes and take a slow, deep breath in through your nose, mentally counting to four as you visualize drawing the first side of the box.
2. Hold your breath as you mentally draw the second side of the box, again counting to four.
3. As you draw the third side of the box, slowly exhale to a count of four.
4. Hold your breath once more, counting to four, as you draw the last side of the box.

Repeat this cycle a few times, focusing on the rhythm of your breath and the image of the box in your mind. You might start to feel a wave of calm washing over you, that's your body's natural relaxation response kicking in.

Box breathing is a great tool because it's simple, discrete, and you can use it anywhere - in the middle of a stressful meeting, in a traffic jam, or during those challenging parenting moments. It's like having a personal stress-relief button at your fingertips.

Another deep breathing technique I often use is *diaphragmatic breathing.* It's about engaging your diaphragm, a large muscle located between your chest and stomach, and getting your whole body involved in the process of breathing. Start by placing one hand on your chest and the other on your stomach. As you breathe in deeply, aim to keep your chest still while pushing your stomach out. As you breathe out, your stomach should naturally fall back. Just like box breathing, diaphragmatic breathing can help trigger your relaxation response, creating a sense of calm and tranquility.

These deep breathing exercises work wonders because they tap into your body's natural ability to relax and reset. They help reduce tension, slow your heart rate, and calm your mind, providing a much-needed break from the surge of anger. Plus, they bring your focus back to the present moment, away from the stressor that sparked your anger.

Remember, the effectiveness of these breathing exercises lies in their regular practice. The more you practice, the more natural they will feel, and the easier it will be to use them when anger strikes. So, next time you feel the storm of anger brewing, give deep breathing a try. It might just become your secret weapon in your battle against parental anger.

Here and Now: Harnessing the Power of Mindfulness

In the midst of the daily hustle and bustle, it's easy to get caught up in our thoughts and emotions, often leading us to react impulsively to challenging situations. But what if we could create a buffer between our feelings and our reactions? This is where mindfulness comes in. At its core, mindfulness is about being fully present in the moment, paying attention to your thoughts, feelings, and sensations without judgment. It is about cultivating a deliberate awareness of the present moment, allowing us to respond to situations with clarity and compassion rather than reacting out of frustration or anger. By practicing mindfulness, we can learn to respond to our children's behavior from a place of calm and understanding, rather than reacting out of frustration or anger.

There are various ways to cultivate mindfulness. One of the simplest ways to begin practicing mindfulness is through mindful breathing. It's similar to the deep breathing exercises we discussed before, but with an added element of keen observation. As you focus on your breath, notice how it feels as the air moves in and out of your body. Pay attention to the sensation of your chest and belly rising and falling. You might even notice the coolness of the air as you inhale and its warmth as you exhale. Mindful breathing anchors you in the present moment and provides a calming refuge from the storm of thoughts and emotions that might be swirling around you.

Body scan meditation is another effective mindfulness practice that can help ground you in the present. Start at the top of your head and slowly move your attention down to your toes, noticing any sensations, tensions, or discomfort along the way. Perhaps you feel a slight ache in your lower back, or maybe your shoulders are tensed up. The aim is not to judge or change these sensations but simply to notice them. This practice can heighten your awareness of physical cues that often precede anger, such as a racing heart or clenched fists, providing you with an early warning system to respond to your rising anger more effectively.

Mindful parenting practices can also be immensely beneficial in managing anger. This might involve truly listening to your child, noticing their facial expressions and body language, and consciously tuning into your own emotions and reactions. It can also be about savoring the joyful moments with your child, like their infectious laughter or their innocent curiosity, allowing these moments to anchor you in the present and foster a deeper connection.

By cultivating mindfulness, you build a bridge between your emotions and your actions, allowing you to traverse the choppy waters of anger with more ease and balance. It's about recognizing that anger is a natural part of parenting, but it doesn't have to control your responses. With mindfulness, you can respond to your child's behaviour and your own emotions with understanding and compassion, fostering a more peaceful and fulfilling parenting experience.

Remember, like any skill, mindfulness takes practice. It's not about achieving a state of constant calm or never feeling angry. It's about becoming more aware of your emotional landscape, understanding your triggers, and learning to navigate your reactions more effectively. So, why not give it a try? The next time you feel the heat of anger rising, take a mindful breath, tune into your body, and observe your emotions without judgment. You might be surprised at the sense of calm and control it brings.

Fill Your Cup: The Importance of Self-Care

As parents, we're often so focused on taking care of our children's needs that we forget to tend to our own. However, self-care is not a luxury; it's a necessity. It's like the oxygen mask analogy on airplanes: you have to secure your own mask before helping others. The same applies to parenting. By taking care of your emotional needs, you ensure that you have the resilience and patience to navigate the ups and downs of parenting with grace.

Self-care is not about being selfish or indulgent; it's about replenishing your emotional reservoir so that you can be the best parent you can be. Imagine trying to water a garden with an empty watering can. It's impossible, right? Similarly, you can't effectively manage your anger or provide emotional support to your children if your own emotional cup is empty.

So, what does self-care look like? It can take on various forms depending on your personal preferences and lifestyle. It might involve physical activities like yoga, jogging, or a peaceful walk in the park. It could be a quiet moment with a cup of tea and a good book, or pursuing a hobby that brings you joy and fulfillment.

For me, journaling has been a profound self-care practice. It provides a safe, private space to express my thoughts and feelings, reflect on my experiences, and gain insights into my emotional patterns.

Consistency is the key when it comes to self-care. It's not about carving out huge chunks of time or planning elaborate activities; it's about incorporating small, nourishing practices into your daily routine. It could be as simple as taking five minutes each morning to practice deep breathing, or spending ten minutes each night writing in a journal. These small acts of self-care can add up over time, helping to cultivate a resilient emotional landscape capable of weathering the storms of anger.

I invite you to take a moment to reflect on what self-care means to you. What activities nourish you? What brings you joy and peace? Remember, there's no "one size fits all" approach to self-care. It's about finding what works for you and making it a non-negotiable part of your routine.

By prioritizing self-care, you're not only enhancing your emotional well-being but also modeling healthy habits for your children. You're showing them that it's important to take care of our emotional health, just as we take care of our physical health. So, remember to fill your cup regularly. Not only will this help in managing your anger, but it will also enhance your overall well-being, leading to a more fulfilling and balanced parenting experience.

Change Your Lenses: The Role of Cognitive Restructuring

Our thoughts hold a powerful influence over our emotions. What we think can shape how we feel, and how we feel can, in turn, dictate how we respond to situations. This is particularly true when it comes to anger. Often, it's not the situation itself that triggers our anger, but our interpretation of it. This is where cognitive restructuring comes into play.

Cognitive restructuring is a technique used in cognitive behavioral therapy that involves identifying and challenging unhelpful thought patterns. Think of it as an emotional detective's work, where you're examining the evidence behind your thoughts, questioning their validity, and searching for more balanced and constructive alternatives.

Let's say your child refuses to do their homework. Your immediate thought might be, "They're going to fail school." This thought triggers a wave of fear and frustration, which can easily escalate into anger. But what if you took a step back and examined this thought? Is it accurate? Is it helpful? Or is it an overgeneralization, a leap from one small incident to a catastrophic outcome?

In cognitive restructuring, you learn to catch these thoughts, question them, and then reframe them. Instead of viewing your child's refusal to do homework as a sign of impending failure, you might consider other possibilities. Maybe they're finding the work too challenging. Perhaps they're tired or distracted. Or maybe they need a different approach to learning.

By shifting your perspective in this way, you're not just reducing the intensity of your anger, but also opening up a space for understanding and empathy. Instead of reacting out of fear and frustration, you're responding with patience and compassion.

Cognitive restructuring isn't about ignoring or sugarcoating the challenges of parenting. It's about viewing these challenges from a balanced perspective, one that acknowledges the difficulties but also recognizes the possibilities for growth and learning.

Remember, cognitive restructuring is a skill, and like any skill, it requires practice. It might feel a bit unnatural or forced at first, but with time, it can become a natural part of your thought process, a powerful tool in your emotional regulation toolkit.

Let me share another example from my own parenting experience. One day, after a long and tiring day, my child threw a tantrum because he didn't want to eat his dinner. My initial thought was, "He's being unreasonable and difficult." This thought stirred up feelings of frustration and anger. But then I paused and reconsidered. Could there be another perspective? Maybe he was tired. Maybe he wasn't hungry. Or maybe he simply didn't like what I had prepared. By shifting my perspective, I was able to respond with more understanding and less anger.

Through cognitive restructuring, you can transform the lens through which you view your parenting experiences. You can move from a place of judgment and criticism to a place of understanding and empathy, not just for your children, but for yourself as well. After all, parenting has its fair share of bumps and detours. But with the right tools and mindset, you can navigate this with resilience, patience, and grace.

Building Your Emotional Regulation Toolbox

In this chapter, we've explored a variety of tools and techniques for managing and regulating anger. Now, think of yourself as an artist about to create a masterpiece. The canvas is your emotional well-being, and these tools are your paints. It's time to gather them together and create your own unique emotional regulation toolbox.

Your toolbox should be as unique as you are. Just as no two parents are alike, no two toolboxes will be either. The techniques that work for me might not work for you, and that's okay. It's not about finding a perfect fit but about exploring and experimenting until you find strategies that feel right for you, that resonate with your personality, your needs, and your parenting style.

In addition to the tools we've discussed—deep breathing, mindfulness, self-care, and cognitive restructuring —there are many other strategies you can include in your toolbox. Grounding exercises, for example, can be particularly useful during moments of intense anger. These exercises involve focusing on your physical surroundings or your body to help you stay present and grounded.

Creative outlets can also be a wonderful addition to your toolbox. Engaging in activities such as painting, writing, playing a musical instrument, or even gardening can provide a therapeutic outlet for your emotions. They offer a way to express your feelings, to channel your energy into something productive and rewarding.

Physical activities like yoga, dancing, or hiking can also be incredibly beneficial. Not only do they provide a physical release for your emotions, but they also trigger the release of endorphins, your body's natural mood lifters.

Your toolbox can also include activities that bring you joy and relaxation. Maybe it's watching your favorite movie, having a coffee in your favorite café, or spending time in nature. Anything that nurtures your emotional well-being can be a tool in your emotional regulation toolbox.

The beauty of building your own toolbox is that it's an ongoing process. As you grow and evolve as a parent, your toolbox can grow and evolve with you. You might discover new tools along the way, or you might find that a tool that once worked for you no longer does. That's completely okay. Your toolbox is not set in stone; it's a dynamic collection of strategies, a reflection of your personal way towards emotional regulation.

Remember, the goal here is not to eliminate anger. Anger is a natural part of our emotional spectrum, and it has its place. The goal is to manage it, to prevent it from taking the wheel and driving our actions. By assembling your toolbox, you're equipping yourself with the means to navigate your emotional landscape with more ease and grace, to respond to the challenges of parenting with patience, understanding, and compassion.

The Key to Mastery: Practice and Consistency

Lastly, remember that mastering these emotional regulation techniques takes time and consistency. Just as a sailor doesn't become adept at navigating stormy seas overnight, you too will need to commit to incorporating these tools and techniques into your daily life. With consistent practice, these strategies can become second nature, equipping you to respond effectively in challenging moments.

Don't be disheartened if you don't get it perfect right away. Each time you try, you're building up your emotional muscles, just like a workout. And before you know it, you'll be navigating those storms like a seasoned sailor. Consider setting aside a few minutes each day to practice mindfulness or deep breathing. Make a commitment to engage in self-care activities regularly, and challenge yourself to reframe your thoughts when you notice negative patterns emerging. It might feel a bit awkward or forced at first, but with time, these practices can become second nature.

Remember, the goal is not to eliminate anger entirely – that's neither possible nor healthy. Instead, the aim is to understand your anger, to navigate it with more awareness and compassion, and ultimately, to foster a deeper connection with your children. Through consistent practice, you'll find that your ability to regulate your emotions in challenging moments will improve, leading to more peaceful and fulfilling interactions with your children.

To sum up, this chapter is all about empowering you with practical tools and techniques to help you sail through the tempests of parenting. I've shared some of my personal strategies and explained the power of techniques like deep breathing, mindfulness, self-care, and cognitive restructuring.

By developing and honing these skills, you're not only improving your own emotional well-being, but you're also creating a more understanding, patient, and nurturing environment for your children. We all face stormy seas from time to time, and with these handy tactics, I have faith that you'll be able to navigate your way through with resilience and grace. So, here's to embracing the exploration, charting your course, and becoming the skilled sailor you're meant to be. Here's to becoming the parent who can navigate the stormy seas, not without fear, but with courage, compassion, and a well-stocked toolbox.

So, anchor yourself with deep breathing, shine a light on your experiences with mindfulness, tend to your needs through self-care, rechart your emotional landscape with cognitive restructuring, and most importantly, practice consistently. You'll soon be navigating the stormy seas of parenting with newfound confidence and calm.

UNMASKING THE HIDDEN

DIGGING DEEPER INTO YOUR ANGER

Parenting is filled with joy and fulfillment, but it's also akin to exploring an intricate labyrinth. This labyrinth, symbolic of our emotional landscape, houses countless twists and turns, unexpected detours, and even unforeseen obstacles. And deep within this emotional maze lies a potent force that often remains obscured, a force that we've all felt but seldom comprehend fully - our anger.

In the previous chapter, we began to peel back the layers of this complex emotion, acknowledging its existence and exploring practical tools to navigate it. But now, it's time to delve deeper, to unearth the hidden roots that feed our anger, and to illuminate the dark corners of our emotional labyrinth.

Unraveling the hidden depths of our anger is no easy feat. It requires courage, perseverance, and a willingness to confront uncomfortable truths about ourselves.

But it's also brimming with potential transformation and profound healing. By diving beneath the surface, we can expose the concealed emotions and beliefs that ignite our anger, opening the door to a significant personal metamorphosis.

This exploration is not just about understanding the *what* and *why* behind our anger—it's about recognizing the *how*. How these hidden emotions and beliefs manifest in our day-to-day interactions with our children, how they shape our parenting style, and how they influence our overall well-being.

But why is it important to delve so deeply? Because understanding the root causes of our anger equips us to confront it more effectively. It's like untangling a complex knot—the more we understand its intricacies, the easier it becomes to unravel. This knowledge doesn't just empower us to manage our anger better; it sets the stage for genuine healing, personal growth, and emotional freedom.

So, as we embark on this chapter, remember: this is about unmasking the hidden, about bringing light to the darkened spaces within us. It's about turning the spotlight inward and daring to explore what lies beneath. It's about fostering an atmosphere of self-discovery, honesty, and vulnerability—an atmosphere conducive to unmasking the roots of our anger and setting ourselves on the path to emotional freedom.

This exploration is a key to unmasking our anger and discovering the hidden path to emotional freedom.

Unveiling My Shadows

As we delve deeper into the labyrinth of our hidden anger, I'd like to share more about my personal life with you. I find it important because my experiences mirror those of many parents, and I hope that in sharing my story, you might find aspects that resonate with your own experiences, lending you the reassurance that you're not alone.

When I first recognized the prevalence of anger as a parent, it was akin to staring at the tip of an iceberg. What I saw was merely a fraction of the whole picture; beneath the surface lay a complex network of emotions and beliefs that I had unknowingly harbored for years.

I remember a time when my anger served as an armor, a protective shield that hid my sense of inadequacy as a mother. It was easier to lash out in frustration than to admit that I felt overwhelmed, that I was struggling to meet the endless demands of parenting.

Then there were moments when my anger was a reaction to fear - fear of not being able to shield my children from the world's harsh realities, fear of them experiencing pain, disappointment, or hardship. This fear often translated into an overbearing need for control, which inevitably led to frustration and anger when things didn't go as planned.

And perhaps most profoundly, my anger was frequently a manifestation of an ingrained belief that I was falling short - that I wasn't doing enough, wasn't being enough for my children. This deep-seated belief led me to set impossibly high standards for myself, and when I failed to meet them (as was inevitable), anger would bubble up as a defense mechanism.

Unearthing these hidden emotions and beliefs was a process of peeling back layers, one at a time. It required honesty, courage, and patience. But with each layer I peeled back, I gained a clearer understanding of my anger's true nature. I saw it for what it was: a cry for understanding, for healing, and for change.

This process of introspection and self-inquiry wasn't always comfortable. It involved confronting parts of myself that I had long ignored, acknowledging feelings I had pushed aside, and challenging beliefs I had held without question. But it was through this process that I began to see the transformative potential of understanding my anger.

I share these aspects of my life with you not because they're unique to me, but because they're universal. They reflect the struggles that many of us face as parents, the emotions we grapple with, and the beliefs we cling to. By sharing my experiences, my hope is that you'll find some solace in knowing you're not alone, and that you'll feel empowered to start your own self-discovery.

Remember, it takes courage to look inward and confront the shadows that lurk beneath the surface. But it's in this act of brave exploration that we find the potential for profound transformation and growth. I still have progress to make, and so do you, and it's through our shared experiences that we can support each other in unveiling the hidden roots of our anger.

The Inner Mirror: The Art of Introspection

As we move forward, we'll need to equip ourselves with the tools and practices that can help us unlock our innermost thoughts and feelings. One such powerful tool is introspection - the art of looking inward.

Introspection, to me, is like holding a mirror to our inner world. It involves taking a step back from our reactions and emotions, observing them without judgment, and understanding their roots. It's this inward gaze that allows us to see beyond the surface of our anger to the hidden emotions and beliefs that fuel it.

Imagine introspection as a quiet dialogue with yourself, a conversation that unfolds within the recesses of your mind and heart. It's an invitation to understand yourself more deeply and to cultivate a sense of self-awareness that can be transformative.

I found journaling to be a potent form of introspection. It became a sanctuary where I could pour out my thoughts, frustrations, fears, and hopes. I used my journal to capture raw emotions, reflect on my reactions, and trace patterns in my behavior. Over time, I began to see my anger in a new light - not as an enemy to be suppressed, but as a messenger to be understood.

But introspection is not one-size-fits-all. You might resonate more with meditative practices, where you quiet your mind and tune into your inner experiences. Or, you may find mindfulness exercises helpful, where you consciously bring your attention to your feelings and reactions in the present moment. And for some, seeking professional therapy can provide a supportive environment for deep introspection, guided by a skilled professional.

The key is to find a method that resonates with you, one that you can commit to and incorporate into your life. Remember, introspection requires time and space - it's not something to be rushed or squeezed into the corners of a busy day. I encourage you to create a dedicated *introspection time* for yourself, a quiet sanctuary where you can explore your inner world without distraction.

Whether it's early in the morning before the house stirs awake, during a quiet afternoon break, or late at night when the day's chores are done, find a time that works for you. Treat this time as sacred, for it's in these quiet moments of introspection that you'll begin to unravel the layers beneath your anger.

Embrace introspection as your ally. It's through this inward reflection that we can start to understand the complexity of our anger, to see the hidden emotions and beliefs that drive it, and ultimately, to nurture a sense of understanding and self-compassion that paves the way for transformation.

The Hidden Emotions: The Undercurrent Beneath Anger

Anger, like an iceberg, often hides much of its mass beneath the surface. When we experience anger, it's usually just the visible part of a complex emotional landscape submerged in our subconscious. Hidden beneath this anger, there are often other emotions at play - feelings like fear, sadness, disappointment, guilt, or even shame.

These hidden emotions can be the real puppeteers, pulling the strings of our anger, often without us realizing it. Our anger may be loud and commanding, but these quieter emotions beneath are the ones truly steering the ship.

One day, I found myself irrationally angry at my eldest son for spilling a glass of milk during dinner. The anger seemed disproportionate to the minor accident. When I took a moment to introspect, I realized that my anger was not really about the spilled milk. Instead, it was masking a deep-seated fear - the fear of not being in control. The chaos of the spill had triggered this hidden fear, and anger was the mask it wore.

So, how can we unmask these hidden emotions? The key is to invite introspection into our moments of anger.

Here's an exercise you can try. The next time you feel your anger rising, take a deep breath and ask yourself, "What else am I feeling?" This question prompts you to look beneath the surface of your anger, to the emotions that might be fueling it.

Were you feeling scared or anxious? Perhaps you were feeling unappreciated or overwhelmed. Maybe there was a sense of disappointment lurking in the shadows. It could even be a cocktail of emotions, all mixed up together. There's no right or wrong answer. The goal is to identify these emotions, to give them a name and bring them into the light.

Acknowledging these hidden emotions can be a powerful step in unmasking your anger. When you recognize and validate these feelings, you're addressing the real issues at the heart of your anger. This valida-tion is crucial. It's a way of telling yourself, "It's okay. It's okay to feel this way. My feelings are valid." This act of self-validation is a significant part of the healing process.

Remember, it's perfectly normal to have these hidden emotions. We all do. They're part of our human experience. But by identifying and acknowledging them, we can start to understand our anger better. And with understanding comes the power to transform our reactions and heal from within. So let's dive deep, unmask these hidden emotions, and set ourselves on the path to emotional freedom.

Examining Beliefs: The Framework of Our Reality

Our beliefs and assumptions can be thought of as the architectural blueprints of our reality. They shape the way we interpret our experiences, the way we perceive the world around us, and most importantly, they shape our responses, including how we express anger. But what happens when these blueprints are outdated or flawed? They can lead us to respond in ways that are incongruous with our true selves.

For a long time, I held onto a belief that, as a mother, I had to be perfect. I thought I had to always know the right answer, never lose my temper, and manage a flawless household while juggling a career. This belief put me under tremendous pressure and was a significant trigger for my anger.

Each time something went wrong, I saw it as a personal failing. A late school drop-off meant I was failing as a mother. A messy house was a sign of my incompetence. In my pursuit of perfection, I had set the bar so high that it was impossible to reach, and each perceived failure fueled my anger.

The turning point came when I started to question this belief. Was it really necessary to be a perfect parent? And what did *perfect* even mean? Was it about never making mistakes, or was it about being loving, supportive, and doing the best I could?

By examining and challenging this belief, I was able to replace it with a healthier one: that it's okay to be an imperfect parent. That it's alright to make mistakes, to not know all the answers, to have bad days. This shift didn't happen overnight, but with time, I found that my anger responses reduced significantly.

Examining your beliefs isn't always easy, but it's an essential step in understanding and transforming your anger. Here's an exercise you can try:

List down your beliefs related to parenting. They could be beliefs about what a good parent should be, about your children, or about yourself as a parent. Once you have your list, go through each belief and ask yourself:

- Is this belief true?
- Is it helpful or unhelpful?
- Where did this belief come from?
- Can I replace it with a more helpful belief?

Questioning and challenging our beliefs is not about blaming ourselves for having them. It's about acknowledging that they exist and choosing to align ourselves with beliefs that support our growth and emotional well-being. So, let's get out our metaphorical magnifying glasses and start examining the blueprints that shape our reality!

Embracing Vulnerability: The Gateway to Healing

Vulnerability, in its essence, is about having the courage to open up—to expose our feelings, our struggles, and to allow others to see us as we truly are. It's about accepting that we don't have all the answers, that we're all works-in-progress, and acknowledging that it's okay, even necessary, to ask for help. In my own path towards understanding and healing my anger, I've found vulnerability to be an invaluable ally. It's been a bridge to healing, growth, and deeper connections with my loved ones.

Let me share a personal experience. There was a time when I felt overwhelmed by my anger and, honestly, by parenting in general. But I kept it all to myself, believing that as a mother, I was supposed to be strong, to handle everything. I thought admitting my struggles would make me look weak.

One day, I reached a breaking point. I shared my feelings with a close friend. I told her about my struggles with anger, my fears of failing as a mother, and my feelings of being overwhelmed. Far from judging me, she empathized with me, shared her own struggles, and offered support. That moment of vulnerability was a turning point for me. It not only brought me closer to my friend but also made me realize that I wasn't alone, that it was okay to ask for help.

Vulnerability is indeed a courageous act. It's like standing in a spotlight, in the center of a stage, exposed. It can feel scary, especially when it comes to our struggles as parents. But there's enormous strength in vulnerability. It's not a sign of weakness but a testament to our courage, our humanity, and our resilience. By embracing our vulnerability, we allow ourselves to be seen and understood, and this can lead to deeper connections with others and with ourselves.

Remember, there's no "right" way to be vulnerable. It might mean opening up to a trusted friend or family member, seeking support from a professional, or simply allowing yourself to fully feel your emotions without judgment. The key is to approach your feelings and experiences with an open heart and mind, to communicate honestly, and to allow yourself to be seen, warts and all.

Embracing vulnerability isn't always easy, but it's a transformative step towards understanding and healing your anger. And remember, each act of vulnerability, no matter how small, is a courageous step towards greater self-awareness and emotional freedom. So, let's muster up the courage to open up, to be vulnerable, and to allow our true selves to shine through.

Healing and Growth

Healing is a journey, not a destination. It's a process of unfolding, of peeling back the layers of anger, fear, and hurt that we've accumulated over time. It's about acknowledging our feelings, confronting the hidden emotions beneath our anger, and challenging the beliefs that no longer serve us. Each step we take, no matter how small, is a stride towards emotional freedom, towards a healthier, happier version of ourselves.

What's beautiful about this is that the benefits extend far beyond us. When we heal, our relationships heal. Our interactions with our children become less about reacting and more about responding with understanding, empathy, and love. Imagine what that would mean for your relationship with your child. Less conflict, more connection. Less tension, more tenderness.

I've seen how my healing has positively influenced my relationship with my children. I'm less reactive, more patient. I listen more and lecture less. Our relationship is far from perfect—after all, perfection isn't the goal—but it's healthier, happier, and more harmonious.

Now, you may be wondering: "How do I start my healing journey?" Well, acknowledging your anger and the emotions beneath it is the first step. But remember, it's okay to seek help. You don't have to embark on this alone. Seeking professional support through therapy or counseling can be a powerful backing. These professionals can provide you with tools, strategies, and insights to navigate the complex terrain of your inner world.

And above all, remember to be patient with yourself. Healing takes time. Growth takes time. Transformation takes time. It may be long and winding, but every step you take is a step towards wholeness. So embrace the process, celebrate your progress, and know that with each stride, you're moving closer to a place of emotional freedom and deeper connection with your loved ones. You're not just healing for yourself; you're healing for your children, for your family, and for the generations that follow.

Embracing Imperfection: The Road to Emotional Freedom

Throughout your reading, you may have noticed that one lesson has been paramount: the importance of embracing imperfection. As parents, we often put pressure on ourselves to be perfect—to have all the answers, to always respond patiently, to always know what to do. But the truth is, there's no such thing as a *perfect parent*. We all make mistakes, and that's okay.

When we let go of perfectionism and embrace our imperfections, we allow ourselves to grow. We learn to extend the same patience and understanding to ourselves that we offer our children. And in doing so, we create a healthier emotional environment for ourselves and our families.

Remember, it's not about *fixing* ourselves or becoming *anger-free*. It's about understanding our anger, learning to manage it, and transforming our relationship with it. It's about giving ourselves the freedom to feel, to make mistakes, to learn, and to grow. And above all, it's about embracing the beautifully imperfect adventure of parenting.

HEALING WOUNDS, FINDING FREEDOM

FORGIVENESS AND LETTING GO

As parents, we often carry heavy burdens. The weight of unspoken words, past hurts, and unmet expectations can quietly seep into our interactions with our children, fueling the flames of anger. But there's a potent remedy to this: forgiveness and letting go.

Forgiveness isn't just a noble act; it's a crucial step on the path to managing parental anger. It doesn't mean forgetting or denying the pain caused. Instead, it's about releasing the grip that these past experiences have on us, thereby freeing us from the shackles of resentment and hurt. By letting go of our anger and choosing forgiveness, we can reclaim our emotional freedom and move forward with a lighter heart.

As parents, we all make mistakes and face challenges that can lead to feelings of guilt, regret, and resentment. These emotions can be directed towards ourselves, our children, our partners, or even circumstances beyond our control. However, holding onto these feelings only fuels our anger, preventing us from experiencing the joy and connection that parenting can bring.

Imagine carrying a heavy backpack while climbing a steep hill. That's what it's like to harbor resentment and unaddressed anger. It slows you down, drains your energy, and makes it harder than it needs to be. Forgiveness is like setting down that backpack. It doesn't change the steepness of the hill or the length of the road, but it allows you to move forward more freely, with less weight holding you back.

The act of forgiveness—whether it's forgiving others or ourselves—can be transformative. It can heal old wounds, mend broken relationships, and pave the way for personal growth and stronger connections with our children. It allows us to break free from the cycle of anger and reactiveness, empowering us to respond to parenting challenges with understanding and compassion instead.

Letting go of resentment and choosing forgiveness doesn't mean that everything becomes perfect overnight. It's requires patience, self-compassion, and continuous effort. But every step you take on this path brings you closer to emotional liberation and a deeper, more harmonious connection with your children.

In this chapter, we'll delve into my personal dealing with forgiveness, explore the power of forgiving ourselves and others, and discuss practical strategies to let go of anger and resentment. The path to forgiveness might not be easy, but I assure you, it's worth it. Because at the end of this path, you'll find something precious—emotional freedom, healing, and a renewed sense of connection with your children. So, let's embark on this transformative journey together. Shall we?

My Personal Battles with Forgiveness

As we venture into the realm of forgiveness, I want to share with you some of my personal struggles and triumphs. Like many of you, I've had my own battles with forgiveness as a parent. There were times when I was trapped in a cycle of self-blame and guilt, unable to forgive myself for losing my patience or for not living up to my own expectations of being the *perfect parent*.

One such incident still stands out vividly in my mind. It was a typical hectic weekday, and I was trying to juggle work deadlines, household chores, and my children's needs. My youngest was going through a particularly difficult phase, refusing to cooperate at bedtime. Exhausted and stressed, I lost my temper and raised my voice more than I would have liked. That night, after the house finally fell silent, I found myself battling a wave of guilt and regret. I kept replaying the incident, berating myself for losing control, for not being more patient.

In those moments of self-reproach, forgiving myself seemed like an insurmountable task. I was caught in the trap of my own expectations, burdened by the illusion of perfect parenting. But I realized that part of being a parent was accepting my imperfections and learning to forgive myself.

There were also instances where I grappled with forgiving others, particularly my children and co-parents. I recall a time when my eldest son, then a teenager, made a decision that led to serious consequences. The situation was fraught with disappointment, fear, and yes, a great deal of anger.

Underneath my frustration, I discovered a lingering resentment towards him for his actions. I blamed him for the chaos that ensued, and this resentment seeped into our relationship, casting a dark shadow over our interactions. The emotional weight of this resentment was not only a heavy burden for me but it also created a distance between us, hindering our ability to connect and communicate effectively.

These personal experiences were challenging, no doubt. But they were also profoundly enlightening. They forced me to confront the anger and resentment I was harboring, paving the way for healing and forgiveness. In sharing these stories with you, my hope is that you see a bit of your own challenges reflected in mine. That you realize you're not alone in your struggles, and that it's okay to stumble and fall. Because it's through these struggles that we learn to stand stronger, guided by self-compassion and the transformative power of forgiveness.

Unleashing the Healing Power of Forgiveness

What is forgiveness really, and why is it so crucial in our quest towards emotional well-being? At its core, forgiveness is an inner shift, a transformative process that enables us to let go of the resentment and anger that keeps us bound to past hurts. But let's be clear: forgiveness does not mean condoning actions that caused us pain, nor does it involve forgetting what happened. It's not about absolving others of their actions or denying our own feelings of hurt and betrayal.

Instead, forgiveness is a conscious choice we make for our own peace of mind and emotional freedom. It's about releasing the tight grip of resentment that serves only to hurt us, like holding onto a burning coal with the misguided belief that it will harm the one who wronged us. When we forgive, we choose to put down this burning coal. We choose to liberate ourselves from the chains of bitterness and anger, and in doing so, we allow healing to occur.

The transformative power of forgiveness extends beyond our own inner peace. It plays a significant role in reducing anger, increasing empathy, and improving our relationships, particularly those with our children.

When we are mired in resentment, we view others through a distorted lens, often clouded by our anger and hurt. But when we begin to forgive, this fog of anger starts to lift, allowing us to see clearly and develop a greater understanding of others' actions and motivations.

I experienced this shift firsthand with my eldest son. As I began to forgive him, I found myself capable of seeing his actions from a different perspective. I could understand his struggles, his fears, and the immense pressure he must have felt. This newfound empathy allowed me to communicate with him better, to approach our discussions with more understanding, and less anger and judgement. Our relationship started healing, transforming into a more compassionate and empathetic connection.

And it all started with forgiveness. This inner shift was the key that unlocked the door to healing and emotional liberation. And while it wasn't easy, the benefits of forgiveness, the peace it brought to my life and our relationship, made every step worthwhile. The power of forgiveness is truly remarkable, and I encourage you, from the depth of my heart, to embrace it in your own path towards managing parental anger.

The Act of Self-Forgiveness

One of the most transformative steps in managing parental anger is learning to forgive ourselves. It's a critical yet often overlooked aspect of forgiveness. As parents, we're incredibly adept at criticizing ourselves. We beat ourselves up for our shortcomings, for not living up to our own expectations or those of others. We might replay situations over and over in our minds, thinking of all the things we could've done differently. This guilt, self-blame, and constant self-criticism only serve to feed our anger, keeping us trapped in a cycle of negative emotions.

It's important to recognize that everyone makes mistakes – it's part of being human, and yes, it's part of being a parent. It doesn't make us bad parents; it makes us real. The goal isn't to be perfect; it's to grow, learn, and do our best for our children. That's where self-forgiveness comes in. It's about acknowledging our mistakes without allowing them to define us.

So, how do we practice self-forgiveness and embrace self-compassion? One way is by reframing our self-talk. Instead of beating ourselves up over a mistake, we can recognize it as a learning opportunity. We can tell ourselves: "Yes, I made a mistake. But that doesn't define me. I can learn from this and do better next time."

Self-compassion also involves letting go of guilt. While guilt can serve as a signal that we've acted against our values, holding onto it doesn't help us or our children. It's like carrying a heavy backpack everywhere we go— it weighs us down and keeps us stuck in the past.

Letting go of guilt is about recognizing that we did the best we could with the knowledge and skills we had at the time. And most importantly, it's about understanding that we are still deserving of love and kindness, regardless of our mistakes.

The act of self-forgiveness is a powerful tool for personal growth and emotional well-being. It allows us to move past our mistakes and focus on the present, where we have the power to effect change. It creates a space for peace within ourselves, reducing our anger and enhancing our capacity to respond to our children with understanding and love.

Remember, you are not defined by your mistakes. You are a loving, caring parent, doing your best in the challenging daily life. Embrace self-forgiveness, practice self-compassion, and watch how it transforms your relationship with yourself and your children.

Forgiving Others

Forgiving others, particularly those who've hurt us, is a complex yet essential part of managing parental anger. It demands patience, understanding, and most importantly, empathy. It requires us to step outside of our own perspective and try to see the world through the eyes of the other person. This doesn't mean justifying their actions or neglecting our own feelings, but it allows us to better understand their actions, and in this understanding, we can begin to find forgiveness.

When we perceive ourselves as being wronged, it's easy to hold onto resentment. However, these resentments become heavy burdens that we carry, exacerbating our anger and affecting our relationships, especially with our children. By practicing empathy and perspective-taking, we can start to release these resentments.

So, how can we develop this empathy and perspective-taking? One strategy involves trying to understand the other person's circumstances and motivations. Were they acting out of fear, stress, or their own unresolved issues? This doesn't excuse their actions, but it can help us see them in a different light.

Honest and open communication is another powerful tool in this process. It allows for a mutual understanding, providing a space where both sides can express their feelings without judgment. It might be challenging and uncomfortable, but it often clears up misunderstandings and facilitates healing.

Remember, forgiveness is not about the other person—it's about freeing ourselves from the burden of resentment. It's a gift we give to ourselves, allowing us to move forward and focus on creating more positive, healthier relationships.

When we forgive, we open a pathway to rebuilding and repairing our relationships, be it with our co-parents or our children. We replace anger and resentment with understanding and empathy, leading to deeper connections and a more harmonious family dynamic.

Forgiveness is a continuous progress. It might take time, and that's okay. What's important is that we're taking steps towards it. So, take a deep breath, summon your strength, and take that first step. You might be surprised at the freedom and peace it brings to your life and your relationships.

Techniques for Releasing Anger and Resentments

While understanding the concept of forgiveness is essential, putting it into practice requires concrete steps and techniques. There are many ways to let go of anger and resentment, but in this chapter, I'd like to share with you some practical exercises that have helped me with to forgive more.

One of the most powerful practices I've found is writing forgiveness letters. This involves writing a letter to the person you're trying to forgive, pouring out all your feelings, frustrations, and ultimately, your wish to forgive them. You don't need to send these letters—it's more about the process of writing them. It's a cathartic exercise that helps you articulate your feelings and facilitates the process of letting go.

Another powerful technique is forgiveness meditation. This practice involves visualizing the person you want to forgive, expressing your forgiveness towards them, and sending them positive thoughts. This might seem hard, especially if your anger is intense, but remember, forgiveness is for you. It's about releasing the burden of resentment for your own peace and healing.

Here's a step-by-step guide for a simple forgiveness meditation:

1. **Find a quiet place:** Look for a space where you can be alone and undisturbed. It could be your bedroom, a quiet corner in your house, or even a peaceful spot in a park.

2. **Begin with calming your mind:** Close your eyes, take a few deep breaths, and allow your body to relax. Feel the tension melting away with each exhalation.

3. **Visualize the person:** Bring to mind the person you wish to forgive. Try to picture them as clearly as possible.

4. **Express your forgiveness:** Silently say to them, "I forgive you. I release my anger." Use your own words that feel right for you.

5. **Acknowledge your feelings:** Notice any emotions or sensations that arise during this process. If you feel resistance or discomfort, that's okay. Recognize these feelings without judgment.

6. **End the practice:** Gradually bring your awareness back to your surroundings. Take a

few more deep breaths, and when you feel
ready, gently open your eyes.

Remember, forgiveness is not a one-time act. You might
need to repeat this exercise several times over days,
weeks, or even months. And that's perfectly okay. The
key is to be patient with yourself and honor your own
pace.

By regularly practicing these techniques, you'll gradually notice a shift in your feelings. The intensity of
your anger may lessen, and you might feel lighter,
freer. This is the power of forgiveness and letting go.

The Freedom of Forgiveness

Forgiveness is more than just a means to manage anger;
it's a doorway to a profound sense of freedom. This
freedom comes from releasing the heavy chains of
resentment that have bound us to past hurts. It creates
room for healing, growth, and the blossoming of more
positive emotions like compassion and understanding.

When I forgave my son for his past actions, I felt as
though a great weight had been lifted from my shoulders. A sense of calm swept over me—a calm that I
hadn't experienced in what felt like forever. It was as if
a fog had been lifted, and I could see the path forward
more clearly.

Our relationship began to heal from that point onward. We started connecting on a deeper level, talking more openly and honestly about our feelings. Our interactions became less about the past and more about the present and future. I noticed a similar transformation in my relationships with my other children and co-parent as well. The practice of forgiveness allowed for a more peaceful dynamic to unfold, and I found myself better equipped to manage my anger.

My personal growth during this time was tremendous. I became more patient, understanding, and compassionate. I learned to listen more and react less. I began to understand that forgiveness was not a destination but a continuous improvement—a path that I needed to walk every day.

Let me be clear: forgiveness didn't make the past disappear. It didn't condone the actions that had caused me pain. But it allowed me to let go of the emotional baggage that I had been carrying around. It allowed me to free myself from the clutches of anger and resentment.

This is the freedom that forgiveness offers. It's an emotional liberation that not only transforms us as individuals but also our relationships, especially the ones with our children. Each step we take towards forgiveness, each resentment we release, each act of understanding we offer, contributes to this freedom. It's a continuous process, a lifelong march, and every step is a step towards a more peaceful, happier you.

Towards a Future of Healing and Connection

I invite you to embrace forgiveness as a pathway to healing and deeper connections. It's not an easy path, but the rewards are immense. You will find peace, not just within yourself, but also within your family. Forgiveness can pave the way for a more harmonious family dynamic, where anger doesn't dictate your interactions, but understanding and love do.

Remember, every step you take towards forgiveness is a step towards a brighter future for yourself and your children. It's a gift you give yourself—a gift of freedom, peace, and emotional liberation. So, let's step onto this path together, navigating the bumps and twists with courage and grace. Because you deserve to feel light, free, and joyful. And forgiveness can help you find that joy.

As you continue, remember that you are not alone. We are walking this path together, supporting and uplifting each other. Let's continue to uncover the layers of our anger, learning, growing, and healing together.

In the next chapter, we'll explore how effective communication can help manage anger and build healthier relationships with our children. Because when we speak from a place of understanding rather than anger, we open the doors to deeper connections and mutual respect. But for now, take a moment to reflect on your own progress towards forgiveness. Recognize the progress you've made and remember to be kind to yourself. After all, this is not about perfection, but about growth, understanding, and above all, love.

6

COMMUNICATION AND CONNECTION

BUILDING STRONGER RELATIONSHIPS

Communication. It's a word we often hear, but its true essence is far more powerful than we realize, especially as a parent. It's the bridge that connects us to our children, that allows us to understand their world, and them, ours. But beyond that, communication is the key to managing our own emotions, including anger, and fostering healthier relationships with our children.

As parents, we're not just caregivers; we're mentors, teachers, and confidants to our children. Our words, our tone, and even our non-verbal cues impact them more than we know. Effective communication can be transformative. It has the power to diffuse tension, resolve conflicts, and deepen our understanding of each other. It enables us to express our emotions healthily and assertively, reducing the chances of anger taking hold.

But communication isn't just about talking; it's about listening, understanding, and connecting on a deeper level. It's about creating a safe, supportive space where our children feel heard, validated, and loved. When we embrace effective communication, we do more than manage our anger; we pave the way for emotional well-being and harmony within our family.

In this chapter, we'll explore the many facets of communication, from assertive expression to empathetic listening, and how we can incorporate them into our everyday interactions with our children. We'll delve into the art of nonviolent communication and how it can strengthen our connection with our children. We'll also look at how communication can turn conflicts into opportunities for growth, and finally, how we can use it to repair and rebuild relationships.

As we embark on this exploration, remember that change doesn't happen overnight. Every step you take brings you closer to your goal of emotional freedom. So, let's begin together, hand in hand, one page at a time.

The Transformative Power of Communication

In the labyrinth of parenting, communication has often served as my guiding light. It's through this lens that I want to share a few personal experiences, times when the power of communication transformed my relationship with my children and helped manage my anger.

One incident that stands out vividly is a struggle I had with my eldest, Max. It was a period of academic challenges for him, especially with math, a subject he was finding particularly hard. Each failed attempt at solving problems amplified his frustration, and as his mother, I found myself mirroring his emotions. One day, after yet another unsuccessful math session, Max, fueled by his frustration, stormed off to his room, slamming the door behind him.

I stood there, feeling my own frustration rising like a tidal wave, threatening to consume me. My mind was a whirlwind of unspoken words and pent-up anger. But somewhere within that storm, a moment of clarity emerged. I realized that letting my anger take the driver's seat would only lead us down a path of more frustration and disconnect.

So, instead of succumbing to my anger, I took a deep breath, allowing a sense of calm to wash over me. I walked up to Max's room and gently knocked on his door, asking if we could talk. I remember the look of surprise on his face as he hesitantly nodded.

We sat down, and instead of lecturing or expressing my own frustrations, I chose to listen. I listened as Max opened up, expressing his own anger, his fears, and his feelings of inadequacy. He shared his worries about falling behind his classmates and his fear of disappointing us, his parents. It was an emotional conversation, but one that needed to happen.

That day, I learned more about my son than I had in months. And as I listened to him, my anger began to melt away, replaced by empathy and understanding. It was a transformative experience, not just for Max, but for me as well. Our relationship began to shift, becoming more open and connected. And most importantly, my anger found a new outlet, one that was constructive and healing.

This experience was a testament to the power of open and empathetic communication. It reminded me that sometimes, all it takes is a pause, a deep breath, and a willingness to listen. This time with Max was a turning point, a moment that underscored the importance of communication in managing my own anger and nurturing a stronger relationship with my children.

Sharing these personal moments with you is not just about telling my story. It's about reminding you that you're not alone in your struggles. It's about creating a connection, one parent to another, reinforcing that the trials and triumphs we experience in our parenting journeys are universal. And above all, it's about highlighting the transformative power of communication, a tool that we all have at our disposal to manage our anger and build stronger, healthier relationships with our children.

Speaking Your Truth: The Art of Assertive Communication

As parents, we often find ourselves walking a fine line between being too passive or overly aggressive in our communication. But there's a middle ground that empowers us to express our needs and emotions effectively without stepping over boundaries or bottling up our feelings. This is where assertive communication comes into play.

Assertive communication is the ability to express your feelings, thoughts, and needs in an open and honest way, while respecting the rights and beliefs of others. It's not about winning an argument or imposing your will on others. Rather, it's about clearly conveying your needs and feelings, while remaining open to a dialogue.

For example, instead of yelling at your child for not doing their chores or giving them the silent treatment, try saying, "I feel frustrated when you don't do your chores because it creates extra work for me." This approach not only communicates your feelings and the impact of their actions but also opens the door for a discussion.

Why is assertive communication so important in managing anger? When we express ourselves assertively, we let out our frustrations in a healthy manner instead of letting them simmer and eventually boil over into anger. It also fosters understanding between us and our children, helping to defuse potential conflicts before they escalate.

But how can we cultivate assertive communication in our parenting? Here are a few strategies:

1. **Use "I" statements:** Express your feelings and needs from your perspective. Instead of saying, "You make me angry when you don't listen," try, "I feel upset when I feel like I'm not being heard."

2. **Practice active listening:** Show your child that you're fully engaged in the conversation by giving them your undivided attention, reflecting back what you're hearing, and asking clarifying questions.

3. **Set clear boundaries:** Clearly communicate your expectations and the consequences of not meeting them. Remember to be firm but fair.

4. **Speak with respect:** Even when you're frustrated or upset, remember to treat your child with kindness and respect. This models the behavior you want them to emulate.

Assertive communication doesn't promise a world without conflicts or disappointments, but it does provide a constructive framework for expressing our feelings and managing our anger. More importantly, it creates a healthier, more respectful environment for our children, showing them that it's okay to express their feelings and needs in a respectful way.

By integrating assertive communication into our interactions, we can manage our anger more effectively, build stronger relationships with our children, and empower them with the skills they need to express themselves confidently and respectfully. It's a win-win for everyone involved.

Tuning In: The Power of Empathetic Listening

Listening is a skill that's often underestimated. As parents, we sometimes fall into the trap of listening to respond, not to understand. We're quick to offer advice, solve problems, or sometimes dismiss our children's feelings as trivial. But empathetic listening – really hearing and understanding our children – can be one of the most powerful tools in our parenting arsenal.

Empathetic listening goes beyond merely hearing words. It involves understanding the emotions, intentions, and needs underlying those words. It's about putting ourselves in our children's shoes, seeing the world from their perspective. When we listen empathetically, we create a safe space for our children to express their feelings, fears, and dreams. This not only helps to diffuse conflicts but also builds trust, understanding, and connection in our relationship with them.

Let's take a look at some active listening techniques that can enhance our ability to listen empathetically:

1. **Reflective Listening:** This involves repeating or paraphrasing what our children say to confirm our understanding. For example, if your child says, "I'm upset because my friend didn't invite me to her party," you might respond, "It sounds like you're feeling hurt because you were left out of the party."

2. **Validation:** This is about acknowledging and accepting our children's feelings and experiences. It's showing them that we respect and value their perspective, even if we don't necessarily agree with it. For example, "I can see why you're upset. It's tough when friends don't include us."

3. **Avoiding Judgment:** When our children share their feelings or experiences, it's important to withhold judgment and criticism. Remember, the goal is to understand them, not to judge them. For instance, avoid saying things like, "You're overreacting," or "It's not a big deal."

4. **Showing Interest:** Encourage further sharing by asking open-ended questions or making comments that show you're genuinely interested in what they have to say. For

example, "Tell me more about how you're feeling," or "That sounds really difficult."

When we practice empathetic listening, we not only manage our own anger more effectively but also help our children learn to express their feelings in a healthy, constructive way. It teaches them that their feelings matter, that they're valid and worth listening to. And most importantly, it shows them that we're there for them, ready to understand, support, and love them, no matter what.

So next time your child wants to talk, try to put these active listening techniques into practice. You'll be surprised at the profound impact it can have on your relationship with your child and your journey towards managing anger.

Bridging the Gap: Nonviolent Communication

Nonviolent Communication (NVC), a concept developed by psychologist Marshall Rosenberg, is a life-changing tool that can transform our interactions with our children. At its core, NVC is about expressing ourselves honestly and receiving others empathetically. It's a compassionate approach to communication that focuses on our common human needs and encourages mutual respect and understanding.

The NVC process involves four key steps:

1. **Observation:** We start by describing what we observe that's affecting our feelings. It's crucial to stick to the facts and avoid any judgment or evaluation.

2. **Feeling:** Next, we identify and express our feelings. It's important to take ownership of our feelings rather than attributing them to others.

3. **Need:** We then express our underlying needs or values that are connected to our feelings. These are universal human needs such as love, security, peace, or understanding.

4. **Request:** Finally, we make a clear, specific, and doable request to meet our needs. It's essential to use positive language and ensure the request isn't a demand.

Let's consider an example. Suppose your child has left a mess in the living room. Instead of reacting in anger, you could use NVC to express yourself: "When I see toys scattered all over the living room (observation), I feel frustrated (feeling) because I need our shared spaces to be tidy and organized (need). Could you please pick up your toys before dinner (request)?"

It's simple, yet powerful. It creates a space for open, honest, and respectful communication. It allows us to express our feelings and needs without blaming or criticizing, and invites our children to do the same. This not only helps to manage our anger but also nurtures connection, empathy, and understanding within our family.

Using NVC doesn't mean we'll never experience conflict or that our children will always meet our requests. However, it offers a roadmap for navigating challenging situations and disagreements in a way that fosters connection rather than distance.

Incorporating NVC into our daily interactions with our children may require practice, but the rewards are worth the effort. As we become more comfortable with this approach, we'll likely find our conversations becoming more empathetic, our conflicts less intense, and our relationships stronger and more connected.

Remember, the goal is not perfection, but progress. And every step we take towards open, honest, and compassionate communication is a step towards a more peaceful, loving, and connected family life.

Conflict Resolution: Learning and Growing Together

As parents, we've all been there: standing in the middle of a conflict with our children, feeling the heat rise in our cheeks and our patience wearing thin. But what if I told you that these moments of conflict could be transformed into invaluable opportunities for growth and understanding?

Conflicts, though challenging, are a natural part of parenting. They're a sign of your child's developing autonomy and a chance for you to guide them towards respectful, constructive communication. Rather than viewing these disagreements as battles to be won, consider them as joint problem-solving opportunities.

The key lies in how we approach these moments of tension. By focusing on win-win solutions, we promote a sense of teamwork and mutual respect. Let's say your teenager wants to stay out past their usual curfew. Instead of an immediate *no*, engage in a conversation. Understand their viewpoint, express your concerns, and work together to find a solution that respects both your needs and theirs. Maybe it's agreeing on a slightly later curfew, with the understanding that they'll keep you updated throughout the evening.

But how do we get from heated conflict to peaceful resolution? Here are some practical strategies:

1. **Pause and Breathe:** When conflict arises, emotions can run high. Before you respond, take a moment to calm yourself. Deep, slow breaths can help lower your stress levels and allow you to approach the situation more rationally.

2. **Listen Actively:** Make sure your child feels heard. Reflect back what they're saying and validate their feelings. This doesn't mean you

have to agree with them, but it shows that you respect their perspective.

3. **Express Yourself Assertively:** Use "I" statements to express your feelings and needs. This helps to prevent your child from feeling attacked and keeps the communication open and respectful.

4. **Find a Win-Win Solution:** Seek a resolution that respects both your needs and your child's. It might require some creativity and compromise, but it's an invaluable lesson in mutual respect and problem-solving.

Teaching our children how to navigate conflicts constructively equips them with crucial life skills. They learn to communicate their needs assertively, understand others' perspectives, and find mutually satisfying solutions. These are skills that will serve them well beyond the family home, in their friendships, future relationships, and professional lives.

Remember, every challenge we face in parenting is an opportunity for growth—for us and our children. As we guide them through the rough seas of conflict, we're helping them learn to sail their own ship, fostering their resilience, understanding, and emotional intelligence.

Quality Time: Cementing the Emotional Bond

In our fast-paced world, finding moments to slow down and truly connect with our children can seem like an elusive goal. Yet, it's these moments that weave the fabric of our relationships, strengthening the emotional bonds that tie us together. Spending quality time with our children not only builds happier, more connected relationships but also significantly reduces the likelihood of anger and misunderstandings.

Let's dive deeper into how quality time plays a role in managing our anger as parents. When we engage in shared activities, we're creating a space for open communication and understanding. We're showing our children that we're interested in their lives and that we value their company. This sense of connection can diffuse tension and foster mutual respect, making it easier to navigate difficult conversations without resorting to anger.

Moreover, shared experiences, rituals, and meaningful conversations with our children can serve as anchor points in our relationships. These shared moments, whether it's a nightly bedtime story, a weekly game night, or daily meals together, provide a sense of stability and predictability that children crave. They become cherished memories, a repository of shared joy and understanding that we can draw upon in times of conflict.

Finding time for these moments amidst our busy schedules might seem daunting, but remember, it doesn't always have to be a grand gesture or a time-consuming activity. Here are a few simple ideas:

1. **Daily Conversations:** Spend a few minutes every day talking about your child's day. Ask open-ended questions that encourage them to share their experiences and feelings.

2. **Shared Activities:** Engage in activities that both you and your child enjoy. It could be cooking, gardening, hiking, or playing a board game. The aim is to enjoy each other's company while doing something you both love.

3. **Establish Rituals:** Rituals provide a sense of continuity and comfort. It could be something as simple as a special breakfast on Saturdays, a weekly movie night, or a bedtime story ritual.

4. **Show Interest in Their Interests:** Take an interest in your child's hobbies, even if they don't align with yours. It shows them that you value their individuality.

5. **Be Present:** When spending time with your child, try to be fully present. Put away your phone and other distractions and focus entirely on them.

Remember, it's not about the quantity, but the quality of time we spend with our children. Even the smallest moments of genuine connection can make a significant impact on our relationships. Through these moments, we're not only strengthening our bonds but also nurturing a sense of understanding and respect, key ingredients in managing our anger and building stronger relationships.

Repairing and Rebuilding: Healing Through Communication

Communication doesn't just prevent or diffuse conflicts; it also has the power to heal. Open and honest communication can repair strained relationships and rebuild trust. It's about acknowledging mistakes, expressing regret, and showing willingness to change.

I remember a time when my anger got the best of me, and I ended up shouting at my daughter, Lily. I immediately regretted it. Instead of letting the guilt consume me, I decided to apologize. I sat down with Lily, admitted my mistake, and promised to do better. That conversation didn't just heal the rift between us, it brought us closer. It showed Lily that it's okay to make mistakes as long as we learn from them and make amends.

Communication in parenting isn't a one-time event; it's continuous learning and practicing. It's about maintaining an open line of dialogue with our children, expressing love, setting boundaries, resolving conflicts, and nurturing connection. It's about creating a family environment where everyone feels heard, understood, and valued.

Reaching emotional freedom as parents isn't always easy. It requires patience, commitment, and a whole lot of self-compassion. But with each step we take, with each conversation we have, we're not only managing our anger but also building stronger, healthier relationships with our children. And that, dear parents, is worth every effort.

7

CHANNELING ANGER

EMPOWERMENT AND GROWTH

Until now, we've explored the intricate labyrinth of anger, peeling back its layers and unmasking its many disguises. Together, we've faced this powerful emotion head-on, gazing into its fiery eyes with courage and determination.

Our quest has led us to this pivotal moment, a turning point in our understanding and relationship with anger. What if we could look at anger not as a foe to conquer, but as an unexpected ally? What if we could transform this perceived adversary into a catalyst for empowerment and growth?

In this chapter, we'll do just that. We will venture into the transformative potential of anger. We'll learn to embrace its energy, harness its power, and channel it into positive action. This is not about suppressing or denying anger. Instead, it's about understanding its nature, listening to its messages, and using it as a tool for personal growth and improved parenting.

Anger, like all emotions, has its purpose. It signals when something isn't right, when boundaries are crossed, or when needs are not met. Rather than letting it control us, we can take charge and use it as a driving force for change. We can turn those fiery feelings into fuel for empowerment, assertiveness, and personal growth.

Understanding and harnessing anger constructively isn't an easy task, but it's a rewarding one. It requires openness, self-awareness, and a willingness to break free from old patterns. But trust me, as we take these steps together, you'll discover that anger can indeed be a powerful ally in your parenting life. This transformative process can lead to stronger relationships with your children, imbued with more understanding, respect, and connection.

Let's uncover the hidden potential of this potent emotion, turning challenges into opportunities and frustrations into fuel for positive change.

Anger: The Misunderstood Emotion in Parenting

As we delve deeper into our understanding of anger, it's essential to recognize that this powerful emotion is not the villain it's often made out to be. Yes, anger can lead to heated outbursts, harsh words, and strained relationships if left unchecked. But at its core, anger is just another emotion, a natural human response to certain situations. It's a signal, an alarm bell that rings loudly when our boundaries have been crossed or our needs unmet.

Let's pause and reflect on this for a moment: Anger isn't inherently bad. It's neither destructive nor harmful by nature. Instead, it's our reaction to it - how we express and manage it - that can result in negative outcomes.

Parenting is laden with moments that can evoke strong emotions, and anger is no exception. Think about the times when your patience wore thin. The forgotten toys strewn across the living room floor. The blatant dismissal from your teenager, met with an eye roll after you shared some well-intended advice. The toddler tantrum in the middle of the grocery store aisle.

It's in these moments that anger can flare up, rising like a fiery phoenix from the ashes of frustration, exhaustion, and sometimes, hurt feelings. The key here is to acknowledge that these triggers exist, and they can provoke anger in even the most patient among us.

However, it's crucial to remember that unchecked anger can cast a shadow over our relationship with our children. It can create a chasm of misunderstanding, resentment, and hurt. A single moment of uncontrolled anger can leave lasting imprints on our children's minds and hearts.

This realization is not meant to induce guilt or fear, but to underline the importance of understanding our anger and managing it constructively. By gaining deeper insight into our anger, its triggers, and its potential impact, we can navigate our parenting lives with increased empathy, patience, and understanding. We can use our anger as a tool for personal growth, positive change, and improved relationships with our children. So, let's take a closer look at how we can do this.

Learning from My Own Anger: A Personal Story

Let me take you back to an ordinary afternoon that became a turning point in my quest of understanding and managing my anger. It had been a particularly stressful day filled with work deadlines, endless chores, and the constant juggle of parenting. My eldest, engrossed in a video game, seemed oblivious to the mounting pressures of the day, completely neglecting his homework.

In my heightened state of stress, I found myself snapping at him, my words sharper than I had intended. The room fell silent as my outburst echoed off the walls. The video game's lively music suddenly seemed muffled, and the look of surprise and hurt on my son's face etched itself into my mind.

Our connection, usually so strong, felt strained in that moment. I could feel the wall of misunderstanding rising between us, my harsh words serving as the bricks and my uncontrolled anger as the cement. My son retreated into his shell, and I was left standing in the aftermath of my anger, a maelstrom of guilt and regret swirling within me.

Once the storm of my anger had passed and calmness descended, I took a moment to reflect. Why had I reacted so strongly? Was it truly about the neglected homework or was there something more beneath the surface of my anger?

Upon introspection, I realized that my anger was a reflection of my own fears and insecurities. The neglected homework was merely the trigger; the real source of my anger was rooted in my fears about my son's future and my responsibilities as a parent. Was I doing enough? Was he taking his responsibilities seriously? Was he prepared for the challenges that lay ahead?

This realization was a breakthrough. It didn't magically erase my anger, but it gave me a new lens through which to view it. I understood that my anger was a signal, a beacon illuminating the deeper concerns that I needed to address.

Armed with this insight, I was able to channel my energy towards addressing the real issue at hand. Instead of allowing my anger to fuel further conflict, I used it as a catalyst for a constructive conversation. I sat down with my son, and we talked openly about responsibility, expectations, and how we could support each other better. This incident was a poignant reminder of how anger, when acknowledged and understood, could serve as a tool for positive change and personal growth.

Managing anger is still a work in progress, but experiences like these have taught me that it's possible to channel anger constructively and transform it into a stepping stone rather than a stumbling block in our parenting daily lives.

The Transformative Power of Anger

Yes, you read it right, *power* and *anger* in the same sentence, and it's not an oxymoron. Anger, often seen as a destructive force, can indeed be transformative when harnessed correctly. It's like fire, which when uncontrolled can cause devastation, but when contained and used mindfully, can forge the strongest of metals.

When we allow ourselves to sit with our anger and explore it rather than pushing it away or erupting, we open a door to personal growth and positive change. Anger can be our compass, pointing us towards issues that we might have overlooked, nudging us to address the elephant in the room.

Think about it this way: anger is like a check-engine light in a car. It alerts us to something that needs attention. It is a signal that something in our life, perhaps in our parenting approach, isn't working as it should. It invites us to pause, take a step back, and examine what's happening under the hood. It's an opportunity for self-reflection and introspection, a chance to delve deeper into our needs, concerns, and fears.

When we respond to anger this way, we can use it as a tool for growth. Instead of letting it lead us into conflict, we can channel it towards understanding and resolution. We can take our anger, born out of unmet needs or crossed boundaries, and let it guide us in refining our parenting strategies.

Imagine a situation where your child's constant refusal to clean up their room triggers anger within you. If you view this anger as a signal, you might realize that it's not just about the messy room but about respect for shared spaces or teaching responsibility. With this insight, you can address the issue at its root, leading to a more effective solution and a more positive parenting approach.

In this light, embracing our anger doesn't mean giving free rein to outbursts. It means acknowledging our anger, understanding its source, and using it as a catalyst for change. It's about turning a potentially destructive emotion into a constructive force that can enrich our relationship with our children and lead to more effective parenting.

Remember, anger is not the enemy. It is a teacher, a guide, a tool for transformation if we're willing to listen to what it has to tell us.

Turning Anger into Constructive Action

Now that we've recognized the potential of anger, let's talk about transforming it into positive, constructive action. It's all well and good to discuss the theory, but it's the practical application that truly makes a difference. Here's how you can channel your anger into productive energy.

When anger surfaces, the first step is acknowledgment. Don't bury it deep down, and don't let it erupt like a volcano. Instead, give yourself permission to feel this emotion. It's natural, it's human, and it's okay. Take a deep breath, feel your feet on the ground, and give yourself a moment to regain your balance.

Once you've done that, it's time for some detective work. Ask yourself, "What's really going on here?" Is it simply about the unwashed dishes, or is it about feeling unappreciated? Is it about the repeated tardiness, or is it about respect for your time and effort? Dig beneath the surface of your anger to identify the root cause. This is where self-awareness becomes crucial.

Now that you've identified the root of your anger, the next step is to channel it into a constructive course of action. This is where self-regulation comes into play.

It's about expressing your feelings and needs without attacking or blaming.

Let's say your child didn't do their homework, sparking your anger. Instead of lashing out, you might say, "When you don't do your homework, I feel worried because it's important for your academic progress." This "I" statement allows you to express your feelings without blaming your child, and it opens the door for a productive conversation.

Consider this a form of emotional alchemy, turning the base metal of raw anger into the gold of understanding and effective action. It's a skill, and like any other skill, it takes practice. You may not get it right every time, and that's okay. The important thing is to keep trying, keep learning, and keep growing.

Remember, managing anger isn't about repressing our emotions; it's about understanding and expressing them in a healthy, constructive manner. It's about using our anger, not as a weapon, but as a tool for building stronger, more understanding relationships with our children.

Using Anger as Fuel for Assertiveness and Advocacy

Harnessing the power of anger can also lead us to become more assertive. This doesn't mean becoming aggressive or confrontational; rather, it means being able to stand up for our own needs and boundaries, and advocate for ourselves and our children in a respectful and effective way.

Let's consider a scenario where your child is struggling with their homework consistently. This could stir up feelings of anger and frustration, which is completely normal. However, instead of allowing these emotions to fuel conflict, you could channel them into assertive action. Your anger could motivate you to communicate with the school, advocating for additional support to help your child succeed academically.

Similarly, let's say you're feeling overwhelmed with the household chores, and it feels like no one is contributing. Instead of allowing your anger to build and erupt, you could use it to assertively express your need for help. You might gather your family and explain, "I've been feeling overwhelmed with all the household chores. I need everyone to pitch in so we can maintain a tidy and functional home." By doing this, you're using your anger to effect positive change in your family dynamic.

The key element in assertive communication is respect – for yourself and for others. It's about expressing your needs, feelings, and boundaries clearly and respectfully. You're essentially saying, "I matter, you matter, and we need to find a way to work this out together."

Remember, being assertive doesn't mean you're being selfish or unreasonable. It means you're acknowledging your own needs while considering others. It's about finding a balance, a compromise that works for everyone. And sometimes, it's our anger that sparks this assertive action, leading us to advocate for ourselves and our children more effectively.

So, the next time you feel anger rising within you, consider how you might use it as fuel for assertiveness. How can it help you express your needs more clearly? How can it inspire you to stand up for your child? And most importantly, how can it lead to a positive change in your family dynamics?

Fostering Emotional Intelligence in Our Children

Understanding and managing anger not only brings about personal growth but can also be instrumental in fostering emotional intelligence in our children. As we learn to navigate our own emotions, we can guide our children to understand and manage their own feelings, including anger, in a healthy and constructive manner.

Children are keen observers and quick learners. They learn a great deal by watching us, their parents. If we demonstrate that it's okay to feel anger, that it's a natural response to certain situations, and that it can be managed effectively, we are teaching them invaluable life skills.

Let's consider a situation where your child is angry because their sibling broke their favorite toy. It's a perfect opportunity to guide them in understanding their feelings. You might say, "I can see you're angry because your brother broke your toy. That's okay. It's normal to feel angry when something you care about gets ruined." This validation of their feelings can help them feel understood and supported.

Next, help them identify what triggered their anger. In this case, it's quite clear – their toy was broken. But as they grow older, triggers might become less obvious, like feeling left out or misunderstood. By helping them identify their triggers, they can better understand their feelings.

Now comes the crucial part – expressing anger respectfully. Teach your child to express their feelings without resorting to name-calling or physical aggression. They might say, "I'm really angry at you for breaking my toy. I wish you would have been more careful."

Lastly, guide them in finding solutions. In this case, it could involve the sibling apologizing and helping to fix or replace the toy. By doing this, you're not only resolving the immediate issue, but you're also teaching your child problem-solving skills.

Remember, by demonstrating healthy anger management, we're equipping our children with the tools to navigate their own feelings. This emotional intelligence will serve them well throughout their lives, helping them build strong relationships and handle challenging situations with grace and resilience. So, as we learn about dealing with our own anger, let's remember to lead by example and nurture emotional intelligence in our children.

The Power of Forgiveness and Repair

Despite our best intentions, there will be times when we stumble and allow our anger to spill over in ways we didn't intend. When we err, it's essential to remember that it's not the end of the world. What matters most is how we respond afterwards. This is where the power of forgiveness and making amends come into play.

After an outburst of anger, it's crucial to take responsibility for our actions and apologize. An apology isn't just about saying "I'm sorry," it's about acknowledging our mistake, expressing regret, and seeking to make things right.

Consider saying something like, "I'm sorry I raised my voice earlier. I was feeling frustrated, but that's no excuse for shouting. I shouldn't have let my anger control me." This not only communicates to your child that you recognize and regret your mistake, but it also models a healthy way to take responsibility for one's actions.

Remember, it's important to be sincere in your apology. Kids are pretty good at spotting a fake apology!

Once you've apologized, work towards repairing the relationship. Discuss what happened, why it happened, and how you can prevent similar incidents in the future. You might say, "I reacted that way because I was feeling stressed, but I'm going to try taking some deep breaths next time or stepping away for a moment when I feel my frustration rising."

Then, reassure your child of your love. Despite your anger, your love for them remains unwavering. Let them know that everyone makes mistakes, and these instances of anger don't define your relationship.

Finally, spend some quality time together to reconnect. This could be as simple as reading a book, going for a walk, or playing a game together. These shared moments can go a long way in healing any hurt and reestablishing your bond.

Remember, by modeling forgiveness and the process of making amends, we're teaching our children valuable lessons about humility, responsibility, and the power of reconciliation. This, in turn, equips them with the skills to resolve conflicts and maintain healthy relationships, now and in the future. So, even in our missteps, there are opportunities for growth and learning – for us and our children.

Channeling Anger Towards Growth: A Recap

You learned the transformative power of anger, uncovering its potential as a catalyst for growth and empowerment. You've explored how you can channel your anger into positive action, advocate for yourself and your children, foster emotional intelligence, and mend relationships through forgiveness and repair.

I want you to remember that your anger doesn't define you. It's simply an emotion, a signal, a tool that, if harnessed correctly, can empower you and promote growth in your parenting journey. So, next time you feel that familiar surge of anger, take a moment, breathe, and remind yourself: "This is an opportunity for growth."

Remember, you have the power to channel your anger towards building a stronger, more understanding, and more connected relationship with your children. You're not alone. We're learning and growing together, turning our challenges into stepping stones towards becoming more emotionally aware and empowered parents.

8

NURTURING EMOTIONAL FREEDOM
SELF-CARE AND WELL-BEING

As we near the end of our mutual mission of unmasking anger and seeking emotional freedom, let's take a moment to appreciate the strides we've made, the lessons we've learned, and the growth we've experienced. This chapter will shed light on one of the most crucial, yet often overlooked aspects of this life-changing experience – nurturing our emotional well-being through self-care. After all, we're not just parents, we're individuals too, deserving of care, compassion, and kindness.

The Value of Self-Care in Parenting

Sometimes, we are so focused on taking care of others that we often forget to take care of ourselves, especially as parents. I know I did. I always found myself at the bottom of my own priority list. The kids, the house, the chores, the family commitments, everything else seemed more important than my own well-being. But as I kept on progressing in my mission to handle my anger and nurturing my emotional health, I realized just how crucial self-care is, not just for me, but for the well-being of my entire family.

I remember days when I would be so engrossed in fulfilling my parenting duties that I would forget to have lunch. Days when I would put off my own health check-ups to ensure my children didn't miss their soccer practice. Days when I would stay up late to clean up the house and wake up tired, only to start the cycle all over again. I was constantly on the move, always caring for others, but seldom for myself. This constant neglect of my own needs led to built-up frustration and resentment, often manifesting as bouts of anger.

I remember snapping at my youngest child, Lily, because she couldn't find her school shoes. My response was harsh, disproportionate to the situation, and it left both of us feeling distressed. I remember the look of surprise and hurt in her eyes and the wave of guilt that washed over me. It was then that I realized that my lack of self-care was not just affecting me, but also my relationship with my children.

This realization was a wake-up call. I began making small changes in my daily routine. I started by setting aside a few minutes each day for deep breathing and meditation. I would wake up a little earlier in the morning to enjoy a cup of coffee in peace before the kids woke up. I made it a point to eat my meals on time, and I started going for regular health check-ups.

As I started to prioritize self-care, I noticed a significant shift in my emotional state. I felt less stressed and over-whelmed. My energy levels improved, and I found myself being more patient and understanding towards my children. I started to respond, rather than react, to challenging situations. My anger was no longer ruling my reactions; instead, I was managing it in a much healthier way.

My children noticed the change too. They saw me as less agitated and more approachable. Our communica-tion improved, and we started sharing more joyful moments together. Looking back, I can confidently say that prioritizing self-care has had a transformative impact on my parenting style and the overall dynamics of our family.

Unpacking Self-Care: It's More Than Just a Spa Day

When I started to incorporate self-care into my routine, I had to first redefine what it meant to me. Self-care is not merely about indulgence or luxury, although those can be part of it. It's about nurturing ourselves in a holistic way - physically, emotionally, and mentally. It's about doing what serves our wellbeing and helps us feel rejuvenated, whether that's a quiet moment with a book, a jog in the park, or a heart-to-heart conversation with a close friend.

In the context of parenting, self-care takes on an even deeper significance. It's about ensuring that we, as care-givers, are taken care of too. It's about recognizing that we can't pour from an empty cup, and we need to refill our own reserves to be the best parents we can be. It's about understanding that our well-being directly influences the well-being of our children.

The first dimension of self-care is physical. It's about nourishing our bodies through balanced nutrition, regular exercise, adequate sleep, and timely health check-ups. It's about listening to our bodies and giving them the care they need. For me, this meant ensuring I was eating nutritious meals, taking short breaks to stretch and move around during the day, and prioritizing sleep.

The second dimension is emotional self-care. This involves acknowledging and expressing our feelings, developing healthy coping mechanisms, and nurturing positive relationships. I found that jour-naling my thoughts and feelings, spending quality time with my loved ones, and seeking professional help when needed were crucial for my emotional well-being.

The third dimension is mental self-care. This includes engaging in activities that stimulate our minds and help us manage stress. For me, this included practices like mindfulness meditation, reading, and taking up hobbies that I enjoyed.

Incorporating these different dimensions of self-care into my daily routine didn't just improve my mood or make me feel good; it had profound effects on my parenting. I found myself more patient, understanding, and responsive to my children's needs. I was better equipped to handle the stresses that came with parenting, and I was able to model healthier behaviors for my children. The benefits were innumerable, making self-care an essential part of my life.

Breaking Down Barriers to Self-Care

Just like me, you might be facing obstacles that make it hard to prioritize self-care. Time is often the biggest barrier we parents face. Between juggling work, chores, parenting duties, and countless other responsibilities, it can seem like there aren't enough hours in the day to take care of ourselves. I've been there, and I've felt the weight of that clock ticking away.

But here's what I learned: self-care doesn't need to be time-consuming. It doesn't have to be an extravagant, hours-long affair. It can be as simple and brief as enjoying a hot cup of coffee while the kids are at school, taking a five-minute mindfulness break amidst your busy day, or reading a chapter of your favorite book before bed. It's not about the quantity, but rather the quality of the time we dedicate to ourselves.

Another common barrier is the feeling of guilt. We often feel guilty for taking time out for ourselves, thinking we are neglecting our children or our responsibilities. I've struggled with this feeling too. But the truth is, caring for ourselves is not selfish; it's necessary. We can't take care of our children to the best of our abilities if we're not taking care of ourselves. It's essential to shift our mindset and understand that self-care is not an act of selfishness but an act of self-preservation.

Then there's the issue of not knowing where to start. With so many aspects of self-care, it can be overwhelming to decide what to incorporate into our routines. What worked for me was starting small. I picked one aspect of self-care that resonated with me and focused on it until it became a habit. Then, I added another, and then another. Gradually, I built a routine that covered the different dimensions of self-care, and that suited my lifestyle and preferences.

Remember, self-care is not a luxury, it's a necessity. And it's not a sprint, it's a marathon. You don't have to do it all at once. Start where you are, do what you can, and remember that any act of self-care, no matter how small, is a step in the right direction. It's achievable for all of us, even in the midst of our hectic lives as parents. You are deserving of care, and it's essential for you to prioritize your well-being.

Your Personal Self-Care Toolbox

When it comes to self-care, there's no one-size-fits-all approach. We're all unique, with different needs, preferences, and schedules, and our self-care practices should reflect that. Here are some practical tips and suggestions that you can tailor to suit your individual circumstances.

To start, identify what rejuvenates you. For me, it's walking in nature, practicing yoga, and getting lost in a good book. These activities help me unwind, refocus, and recharge. What activities make you feel good? It could be anything from painting, cooking, gardening, to even dancing around the living room. The key is to find what resonates with you and makes you feel relaxed and refreshed.

Next, try to incorporate these activities into your daily routine. It doesn't have to be a big chunk of time; even a few minutes can make a difference. For example, you could start your day with a short meditation or yoga session, take a quick walk during your lunch break, or unwind with a book before bed. Be flexible and adjust your routine as needed. Self-care should be a source of joy, not another task on your to-do list.

It's also important to consider different types of self-care. Physical self-care is crucial, but don't forget about emotional and mental self-care. This could involve journaling your thoughts and feelings, practicing mindfulness, seeking therapy or counseling, or simply taking time to relax and do nothing. Mental and emotional self-care can often have a profound impact on our overall well-being.

Remember to listen to your body and mind. If you're feeling particularly stressed or tired, it might be time to step up your self-care practices. Conversely, if you're feeling good, don't skip self-care just because you think you don't need it. Self-care is a preventive measure, not just a remedy. It's about maintaining our well-being, not just restoring it.

Creating your personalized self-care toolbox is about exploring and experimenting. Try different activities, adjust your routine as needed, and remember that self-care is a dynamic process. It's not about what you do, but how you feel while doing it. So go ahead and start building your self-care toolbox. I can't wait to hear about what you discover.

Crafting Your Personal Self-Care Routine

Creating a self-care routine that fits into your everyday life might seem like a tall order, especially with a plethora of responsibilities as a parent. But trust me, it's not only possible, it's essential, and I'm here to guide you every step of the way.

The first step is to reflect on your own needs. What areas of your life feel neglected? Are you always physically tired? Do you often feel emotionally drained? Or perhaps your mind feels like it's in a constant state of chaos? Once you've identified your needs, you can tailor your self-care routine to address these areas.

Next, consider your daily schedule. Look for small pockets of time that you can dedicate to self-care. Remember, self-care doesn't need to be time-consuming. Even just a few minutes can make a significant difference. Perhaps you could wake up 15 minutes earlier to enjoy a quiet cup of coffee, or take a short walk during your lunch break. Maybe you can dedicate a few minutes before bed to meditation or reading.

Once you've identified your self-care activities and the times you can do them, start incorporating them into your routine. Begin with just one or two activities, then gradually add more as you become comfortable with your new routine. Remember, the goal isn't to add more tasks to your to-do list; it's to create a routine that nourishes and rejuvenates you.

Here's a tip: write down your self-care plan. Having a visual reminder can be a powerful motivator and can help keep you on track. Plus, it's always satisfying to tick off tasks once you've completed them.

Remember, your self-care routine should be flexible and adaptable. Some days, you might have more time for self-care than others. That's perfectly okay. Adjust your routine as needed, and most importantly, be gentle with yourself. You're doing the best you can, and that's enough.

Creating a self-care routine is an act of self-love. It's a commitment to prioritizing your well-being amidst the hustle and bustle of parenting. And remember, taking care of yourself isn't selfish; it's necessary. After all, you can't pour from an empty cup. So, start crafting your self-care routine and fill your cup to the brim. You deserve it.

The Link Between Self-Care and Emotional Freedom

When we think about self-care, we often focus on its immediate, tangible benefits - feeling relaxed after a hot bath, the sense of calm from a meditative session, or the invigoration from a brisk walk. While these perks are indeed valuable, the true power of self-care lies in its profound impact on our emotional health and freedom.

Self-care and emotional freedom are intricately connected. To understand this, let's first define what emotional freedom means. It's the ability to under-stand, manage, and express our emotions in a healthy way. It's about being resilient in the face of emotional turmoil and being able to bounce back from emotional setbacks. And how does self-care contribute to this? Let's delve into that.

When we engage in self-care, we create a space for ourselves where we're attending to our needs - be it physical, emotional, or mental. This act of nurturing ourselves sends a powerful message to our brain that we matter, that our well-being is important. This, in turn, boosts our self-esteem and emotional resilience, giving us the strength to face life's challenges, including our struggle with anger.

Self-care practices like meditation, mindfulness, physical exercise, or even simple acts like reading a good book or enjoying a cup of tea, allow us to connect with ourselves. They provide us with an opportunity to check in with our emotions, to understand them rather than suppress them. This understanding is the first step towards emotional freedom.

Moreover, self-care contributes to emotional balance. Regular self-care practices can lower stress levels, reduce anxiety, and enhance our mood, enabling us to handle our emotions better. When we're less stressed, we're less likely to react impulsively, and more likely to respond thoughtfully - a key aspect of managing anger.

Now, here's the part that brings it all together for us as parents. When we're emotionally balanced and resilient, we create a harmonious environment for our children. Kids are incredibly perceptive and often pick up on their parents' emotional states. By managing our emotions better, we're not only modeling healthy emotional habits for our children, but we're also creating a more peaceful, positive home environment.

So, you see, self-care is not an indulgence; it's a path to emotional freedom. By taking care of yourself, you're nurturing your emotional well-being, promoting resilience, and contributing to a more harmonious family life. And remember, your emotional freedom is not just a gift to yourself, but to your family as well.

Teaching the Art of Self-Care: A Lesson for Our Little Ones

As we progress through the experience of raising our children, we often forget that our actions speak louder than our words. Our children are observing us, soaking in our behaviors and attitudes like tiny sponges. This is why it is so crucial that we model self-care for them. By doing so, we teach them an invaluable lesson - that taking care of one's well-being is not a luxury, but a necessity.

When we practice self-care, we show our children that it's important to prioritize our needs, and that it's okay to take time out for ourselves. This goes a long way in promoting healthy self-esteem in our children. They learn that their needs matter and that it's essential to respect their own well-being.

But how exactly do our children learn from us? Well, imagine your little one seeing you take a few minutes every morning to meditate or write in your journal. They might not understand the intricacies of these practices, but they notice that you're taking time for yourself. They learn that it's a part of your routine, something that you value. And over time, they'll start to imitate you, incorporating their own versions of self-care into their routines.

However, it's not just about passive learning. We can actively involve our children in self-care activities and use these moments to teach them about well-being. For instance, we can invite them to join us on our morning walks or have them participate in a family yoga session. We can encourage them to explore activities that they enjoy, be it painting, playing an instrument, or spending time in nature.

While involving them, it's important to explain why we're doing what we're doing. Talk about how these activities make us feel, how they help us relax and recharge. Discuss the concept of emotional well-being and how taking care of ourselves contributes to it. Remember, the goal is not just to teach them the activities, but to help them understand the value of self-care.

Incorporating self-care into our parenting also provides us with opportunities to have open conversations about emotions and stress. We can talk about how certain days might be tough and how self-care can help us navigate those days. By doing so, we not only teach them coping mechanisms, but we also normalize conversations about emotional health, paving the way for them to openly discuss their feelings and challenges as they grow older.

Modeling self-care for our children is one of the most powerful lessons we can impart. It not only contributes to their immediate well-being but also equips them with a skill that will serve them well throughout their lives. As parents, our goal is to raise healthy, happy, and resilient children, and teaching them the art of self-care is a significant step in that direction.

Letting Go of Guilt

In the parenting journey, guilt seems to be an ever-present companion. It sneaks in when we least expect it, making us question our choices and actions. And when it comes to self-care, that guilt can be particularly persistent. How many times have we thought, "I shouldn't be doing this for myself when there's so much to do for the kids," or "I'm being selfish for taking this time out"?

If you've had such thoughts, believe me, you're not alone. I've been there too. But over time, I've learned that this guilt, while completely natural, is undeserved and counterproductive. It hinders us from fully embracing self-care and reaping its benefits. And that's something we need to change.

Firstly, let's address this feeling of being "selfish". We need to remember that self-care is not selfish; it's self-preservation. It's about refilling our own cup so that we can pour into others. It's about recharging ourselves so that we can be the best versions of ourselves for our children. When we're well-rested, emotionally balanced, and mentally at peace, we're more patient, more understanding, more present. So, by taking care of ourselves, we're actually better equipped to care for our children.

Now, how do we overcome this guilt? One strategy that worked for me was reframing my thoughts. Instead of seeing self-care as taking away from my family, I started viewing it as something that adds to my family's overall well-being. Whenever the guilt crept in, I would remind myself of all the ways my self-care practices benefit not just me, but my entire family.

Another effective strategy is to start small. If taking an hour for yourself feels too much, start with fifteen minutes. Over time, as you notice the positive impact of these moments on your well-being and your parenting, the guilt will start to fade.

It's also essential to communicate with your family. Let them know why you're taking this time for yourself and how it helps you. When our children and partners understand the importance of self-care, they're more likely to support us, which can significantly reduce feelings of guilt.

Remember, guilt is an emotion, and like all emotions, it's neither good nor bad. It's what we do with it that matters. We can let it ruin our self-care progress, or we can acknowledge it, understand it, and then let it go.

Prioritizing self-care might feel uncomfortable at first, especially if you've been sidelining your needs for a while. But as you gradually incorporate it into your routine, you'll notice the profound impact it has on your well-being and your relationships. You'll find yourself more balanced, more resilient, more at peace. And most importantly, you'll be modeling healthy habits for your children, teaching them the importance of self-care, and setting them up for emotional success. So, let's say goodbye to guilt and hello to self-care!

Creating your Perfect Self-Care Plan: A Step-by-Step Guide

Just like it takes time to manage anger and achieve emotional freedom, incorporating self-care into our lives is a process. It's not something that happens overnight. There will be days when you won't find the time or the energy for self-care, and that's okay. What's important is that you continue to strive towards it.

Here are some steps to guide you:

1. **Reflect on Your Needs:** What makes you feel good? What activities relax and rejuvenate you? These are the activities you'll

want to incorporate into your self-care routine.

2. **Identify Opportunities for Self-Care:** Look at your daily routine and identify pockets of time that can be used for self-care. Maybe it's early in the morning before the kids wake up, or perhaps it's during their nap time. Remember, self-care doesn't have to take hours. Even a few minutes can make a big difference.

3. **Make a Commitment:** Once you've identified your self-care activities and opportunities, make a commitment to yourself. Write it down, schedule it in your calendar, do whatever works for you to make this commitment real.

4. **Start Small and Gradually Build Up:** If you're new to practicing self-care, start with small, manageable activities. As you become more comfortable, you can gradually incorporate more self-care activities into your routine.

5. **Be Flexible and Forgiving:** Understand that there will be days when self-care just isn't possible, and that's okay. Don't beat yourself up over it. Remember, this is a journey, not a destination.

By following these steps, you'll be well on your way to incorporating self-care into your routine and reaping the many benefits it has to offer.

The Power of Self-Care: More Than Just a Buzzword

In conclusion, self-care is more than just a buzzword or a trendy concept. It's a vital aspect of our overall well-being and plays a crucial role towards managing anger and achieving emotional freedom. It empowers us to be better parents and role models for our children.

I encourage you to embrace self-care. Prioritize your well-being. Give yourself the same love, care, and attention that you give your children. Remember, you can't pour from an empty cup. By nurturing yourself, you're not only becoming a better parent but also creating a more harmonious and loving environment for your family.

Remember that it's okay to take time for yourself. It's okay to prioritize your needs. You deserve it, and so do your children.

CONCLUSION

As you come to the end of your reading, it's a fitting time to pause, reflect, and summarize the key insights and learnings you've unpacked throughout this book. We've traversed a wide landscape, from understanding the nature of parenting anger to peeling back its many layers, unmasking its roots, and discovering the hidden path to emotional freedom.

This has been a profound exploration of the many facets of parenting anger. We've uncovered layers of understanding, connected with the roots of our emotions, and equipped ourselves with practical tools for managing the fiery feelings that can sometimes consume us.

Let's look back at the key insights we've gathered along the way. In Chapter 1, we validated the universality of anger in parenting. It was a gentle welcome, a reminder that you're not alone, and that it's okay to feel over-whelmed at times.

We peeled back the layers in Chapter 2, unmasking the roots of our anger. We delved into how past experiences and unresolved issues can fuel our fiery emotions, and we introduced the transformative practice of self-reflection. While challenging, it is a powerful starting point for change.

In Chapter 3, we explored practical tools for emotional regulation. We equipped ourselves with strategies such as deep breathing exercises, mindfulness practices, and self-care activities. We emphasized the importance of developing a personalized toolkit of coping mechanisms that align with your unique needs.

Chapter 4 led us deeper into our emotions, inviting us to face the hidden beliefs and feelings fueling our anger. The courage and vulnerability this requires are not to be underestimated, and neither are the transformative effects of such introspection.

Chapter 5 guided us on the healing power of forgiveness and letting go. We faced the reality that to move forward, we must first release the past, a process that requires a compassionate understanding of ourselves and others.

In Chapter 6, we underscored the impact of effective communication in managing anger and building healthier relationships. We discovered that when we communicate with empathy and assertiveness, we foster a connection that can weather even the stormiest emotional outbursts.

Chapter 7 revealed the transformative potential of anger, showing us how this powerful emotion can be channeled into personal empowerment and positive change. We saw how our anger, rather than being an obstacle, can be an opportunity for growth.

Finally, in Chapter 8, we recognized the critical importance of self-care and well-being in maintaining emotional balance and creating a harmonious family environment. We understood that nurturing ourselves is not a luxury but a necessity for our emotional freedom.

Each of these chapters, each of these insights, is interconnected, forming a comprehensive roadmap towards better managing our parenting anger. We've went from validation to exploration, from regulation to introspection, from forgiveness to communication, from transformation to self-care. It doesn't end here, though. Each day offers a new opportunity to apply these insights, to grow, and to nurture the emotional freedom we've been seeking.

It has not just been about the information and insights in this book. It's also been about my personal journey – a journey of growth and transformation in managing anger as a parent. As I've shared with you, there have been many bumps along the way, moments of doubt, and times when my anger felt overwhelming. But each challenge, each moment of frustration, has been a stepping stone on my path to emotional freedom.

And what a journey it has been, my friends. An adventure that you have joined me on, and for that, I'm profoundly grateful. Your dedication to becoming emotionally free parents, your willingness to face your anger and peel back its layers – these are testaments to your strength and commitment. They are reflections of your love for your children and your desire to create a harmonious, loving home.

Remember, change is possible. You have the power to create a calmer and more harmonious family dynamic. It may take time, patience, and practice, but each step you take towards understanding and managing your anger is a step towards a happier and more peaceful home.

As we part ways, I want to leave you with some final words of encouragement. Parenting is not about perfection; it's about progress. It's about learning, growing, and doing the best we can for our children and ourselves. And so, as you continue through your challenging daily life, remember to be kind to yourself. Embrace your imperfections. Celebrate your victories, no matter how small. Each one is a testament to your dedication, your resilience, and your love.

Remember that you are not alone. There are countless parents out there who are traveling a similar path, who are experiencing the same struggles and asking the same questions. Reach out to them, share your experiences, and learn from theirs. Together, we can support each other in our quest for emotional freedom.

Keep these strategies and techniques you've learned in this book close to your heart. Draw on them in times of calm and chaos alike. They are your tools, your guideposts, your stepping stones on this path towards understanding and managing your anger.

My heartfelt wish for you, dear reader, is that you continue to grow, to learn, and to discover the joy that comes from mastering your emotions and cultivating a loving, peaceful family environment. You have embarked on a courageous quest, and for that, you should be immensely proud.

Embrace self-compassion and continuous learning in your parenting life. Be gentle with yourself when you stumble and remember that every step, forward or back, is part of it. Keep learning, keep growing, and remember that every day is a new opportunity to become a better parent.

In closing, I want to express my optimism for your future and the positive impact you can have on your families. The strategies and insights we've discussed in this book are not just theoretical concepts; they are practical, actionable steps that can transform your parenting experience. Apply them, adapt them, make them your own, and witness the transformative power of becoming a calmer, happier parent.

Writing this book has been incredible. I'm grateful to have shared this part of my life with you. Your trust, your engagement, and your commitment to becoming the best parent you can be are truly inspiring.

Take each day as it comes, embrace the chaos, the laughter, the tears, and the tantrums. Remember, every challenge is an opportunity for growth, and every stumble is a chance to get back up stronger.

Hold close to your heart the knowledge that your feelings of anger are not a sign of failure but a common part of the human experience. Your willingness to confront these feelings, to understand their roots, and to work towards managing them more effectively speaks volumes about your strength and dedication as a parent.

As you move forward on your parenting odyssey, I encourage you to continue reflecting on the strategies and insights we've explored together. Revisit these pages whenever you need a reminder, a boost of confidence, or just a moment of reassurance that you're not alone in your struggles.

Remember the power of self-care and don't neglect your well-being. You can't pour from an empty cup, and by taking care of yourself, you're not just nurturing your emotional freedom but also creating a more harmonious family environment.

Stay connected with your children, your partner, and your community. Share your experiences and listen to the experiences of others. We learn so much from each other, and your experiences and discoveries could inspire someone else.

And finally, never forget the transformative power of love and forgiveness - for others and for yourself. Be gentle with yourself when you make mistakes, forgive quickly, and love deeply. Parenting is an ongoing process, and it's infinitely more rewarding when we approach it with an open heart.

From the bottom of my heart, thank you for joining me. It's been a privilege to share my experiences and insights with you, and I hope that they have brought you some measure of comfort and empowerment.

Remember, you have the power within you to overcome your anger, to foster stronger connections with your children, and to create a family environment filled with love, understanding, and harmony. I am rooting for you every step of the way.

Wishing you love, peace, and joy,

Sarah Thompson.

A Personal Request from the Author

As a self-published author, your feedback means the world to me. Hearing from readers like you not only helps me grow as a writer but also helps other parents find this resource when they need it most. If you found "Anger Unmasked for Parents" helpful, I would be incredibly grateful if you could take a few moments to leave an honest review on Amazon. Your words could guide other parents to the support and strategies they need to manage their anger and find emotional freedom. Your voice truly matters and can make a difference in the lives of other families. Thank you from the bottom of my heart for your support and for joining me on this journey. Together, we are creating a community of emotionally free parents, nurturing healthier and more harmonious family environments.

Scan to leave an honest review

ABOUT THE AUTHOR

Sarah Thompson is a devoted parent to three beautiful children and an author whose words resonate with warmth, empathy, and authenticity. As a parent who has navigated the tumultuous waters of anger, she brings firsthand experience and a deep understanding of the challenges faced by parents everywhere. Her journey in managing her own anger and finding emotional freedom has been the driving force behind her desire to help others on their own path to emotional balance. Sarah's writing style is highly relatable and engaging, combining her personal experiences with research-backed practices to provide practical, actionable strategies for managing anger. Her book, "Anger Unmasked for Parents" is not only a reflection of her own growth and transformation but also a testament to her dedication to supporting other parents on their journey towards emotional freedom and healthier family dynamics. Sarah is a beacon of hope and a source of inspiration for parents seeking to navigate their own emotions and create a calmer, more harmonious family environment.

Made in United States
North Haven, CT
19 September 2023

41723032R00096